American
Composers

ELSA Z. POSELL

Illustrated with photographs

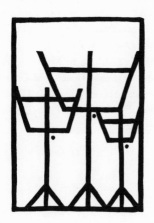

HOUGHTON MIFFLIN COMPANY BOSTON

to JACQUES

ACKNOWLEDGMENTS

In grateful appreciation for their patience, encouragement, and musical wisdom, the author here expresses gratitude to: Klaus G. Roy, composer, director of publications and program book editor of the Cleveland Orchestra; Arthur Loesser, head of the piano department of the Cleveland Institute of Music; Louis Lane, associate conductor of the Cleveland Orchestra; and to Herbert Elwell, distinguished composer and music critic of the *Plain Dealer*.

Members of the staffs of the following libraries have been most helpful and cooperative: the Fine Arts Division of the Cleveland Public Library, the Music Division of the Free Library of Philadelphia, and the Library of the Conservatory of Music of Oberlin College.

For pictures, the author's gratitude to Mrs. Charles E. Ives, for a picture of her husband, Mr. Oliver Daniels, Director of Contemporary Music, Broadcast Music Inc., Boosey and Hawkes, Inc., Carl Fischer, Inc., G. Schirmer, Inc., the Cleveland Press, the Cleveland *Plain Dealer*, and the management of the Cleveland Orchestra.

America and Her Music

AMERICA's development into one of the great musical centers of the world is probably rooted in the growth and development of the country itself and the people who settled here. From France, England, Spain, Holland, and Sweden they came, bringing with them their customs, habits, and traditions many centuries old. These were the foundations of the culture of the new nation, just as the hymns, tunes, dances, and the musical instruments the settlers brought with them were the foundation for their musical development.

Music of the Early Settlers

Not all the early settlers felt the need for music in the new country. The Puritans, who came to New England, believed that music for pleasure was sinful and that musical instruments were instruments of the devil! They did, however, allow music at their church services, but there only the men could sing while the women sat in silence. The heathen Indians were not permitted to sing at all, but they might join in the "Amen" at the conclusion of the hymn.

Despite this attitude on the part of the Puritans, music did creep into their lives without their realizing it. The very first music book to appear in the new country was printed in New England. This was the *Bay Psalm Book*, published in 1640, which contained originally only the words to the psalms. When the book was reprinted for the ninth time, in 1698, music for thirteen of the tunes was included in the back of the book.

The Southern colonists had an entirely different view of music. They considered it pleasant and comforting after long hours of work. The older people taught their children the singing games, dances, and the songs they knew, and their parties and social gatherings were gay affairs in which music played an important part. To them, music was a cultural art. It became the custom for young ladies to learn to sing or play, and every ship arriving in the South brought, whenever space would permit, harpsichords, violins, organs, and other musical instruments.

By 1720 the musical development of the country was already evident. Instruction books on singing appeared, followed by books of favorite songs. Singing teachers were busy, and some of the first music schools were established for the purpose of training church singers. Singing societies were organized in many parts of the country, and some of them are still in existence today. Music was becoming an active and an important part of the community.

Josiah Flagg, an enterprising Bostonian, started to manufacture the harpsichord and the spinet in 1769. This resulted in wide interest, for now instruments were available to anyone in the country who wanted one and who could pay the price. Boston, Charleston, New York, and Philadelphia became the music centers of the new country. By 1829, over 2500 of these instruments had found their way into private American houses.

Celebrated musicians came to the new country from different parts of the world, bringing with them good musical training and instruments. Some gave performances and returned to the places they came from; others remained and became teachers and performers for eager pupils and audiences here. New Orleans built an opera house, in 1808, in which operas in French were performed. The great Handel and Haydn Societies were organized in 1815. America was growing and becoming a musical nation!

Sources of American Music

Although the roots of American music can be traced to the backgrounds of the many different people who settled here, there is much that was particularly American created by the newcomers, their children, and grandchildren. They took the music of the Negro, the American Indian, the folk songs that grew out of struggling pioneer days, the songs and legends of the mountains and forests, and gave a true musical heritage to the American people.

Music tells our story as well as any history book. Like people the world over, Americans found that music expressed for them many things that were difficult to say in other ways. Songs expressed gratitude for good crops and for safety from unfriendly Indians, and eased such back-breaking tasks as chopping trees. Americans sang when they were happy and when they were sad, and every important event was recorded by a song.

When the colonists established their own country, patriotic songs were born. Other songs tell of the westward movement of the early settlers, the building of the railroads, of the Negro slaves working in the cotton and tobacco fields, of lonesome cowboys in windswept prairies, and of the hard life of the lumberjacks in the deep dark woods. America was singing as it worked!

American Music Today

Not too long ago we heard over and over again that America was too young a country to have produced many composers. We looked to Europe for music, as well as for the training of our musicians and especially of our composers. Today the picture is somewhat different; our symphony orchestras are filled with native-born and native-trained musicians, and we have produced many fine composers. Though we must admit that many of them in the past received their training from outstanding European teachers, this picture, too, is changing.

Our own conservatories and universities have become excellent training centers, and our own composers are encouraged through scholarships, grants, prizes, and fellowships to have at least brief periods of freedom to compose without the nagging responsibility of finances. The result is an excellent group of composers who have written a very large number of works.

It is perhaps too early to say how many American composers will survive the rigorous test of time. We have no way of knowing how many of the composers writing in America today will have works played a hundred years from now alongside such timeless composers as Mozart, Beethoven, or Schubert. One thing, however, is certain: when names of great composers are mentioned at that time, included among them will be some of the people who are composing today.

Few composers in America or in Europe earn sufficient funds from their writing to support themselves and their families. Since composers depend on royalties, which they receive each time their music is purchased or performed, their financial return is small. Thus, to supplement their incomes, the great majority of our American composers teach in colleges and conservatories. Many of them, like William Schuman, Howard Hansen, and Peter Mennin, have important administrative positions in the field of music, but all of them devote as much time as possible to composing.

The task of writing a book about American composers is a difficult one because of the problem of selecting composers to be included. There are hundreds of American composers writing good music, but to include all of them in one book would be impossible. Their omission is by no means any indication that they are not equally as important as composers whose names are found here.

The term "American composer" includes in this book not only those composers who were born in America, but also those who came from other lands to find new homes in America, and who have written their major works in this country. But "American composer" is also an open term, for every day musicians are composing new and important American music.

Samuel Barber

born in West Chester, Pennsylvania, March 9, 1910

PENNSYLVANIA-BORN SAM BARBER knew at a very early age that he wanted to be a musician. His doctor-father had hoped his son would follow in his footsteps, but both his mother, who was a talented pianist, and his aunt Louise Homer, a renowned singer with the Metropolitan Opera, aided and encouraged his interest in music. Thus music proved to be the stronger influence and Sam Barber became a musician.

His childhood was a most happy one, spent in a large rambling old house full of good books, music, and many interesting visitors.

Amid these pleasant surroundings, he began to study piano at the age of six and, by the time he was seven years old, had written his first composition. He called it "Sadness." By the time he was ten, he had composed an opera, *The Rose Tree*, to a story written by the family cook.

While still in high school, Sam Barber entered the newly opened Curtis Institute of Music, where he majored in composition, piano, and voice. He was one of the very few students there who was permitted to major in three different subjects.

During his high-school years Sam Barber spent every

Friday in Philadelphia — lessons at Curtis in the morning, followed by concerts of the Philadelphia Orchestra in the late afternoon. (His father, as head of the school board, had made the ruling that any West Chester high-school pupil who was a composition student could be excused from school on Fridays for lessons and Philadelphia Orchestra concerts.)

By the time he was eighteen, Sam Barber had won the Bearns Prize in composition, the Guggenheim Fellowship and the Prix de Rome. This last prize enabled him to go to Europe, where he was free to devote all his time to composition. In the four years it took to complete his studies at the Curtis Institute of Music, he became an accomplished composer, pianist, and singer.

From the very beginning, Mr. Barber's music attracted attention and was performed in America and in Europe. One of his earlier works, "Dover Beach," for voice and string quartet, was a great success and was recorded with Sam Barber himself as baritone soloist. His first major work for symphony orchestra, entitled *School for Scandal*, was performed by the Boston Symphony Orchestra and by almost every other major orchestra in the country.

Today Mr. Barber is probably the best-known American composer. Most of his works have been performed in Europe, and over half of all the works that he has written have been recorded. Unlike many other American composers, his works are not regional, nor are they based on American folk themes or folk songs. His music is sincere and full of moving beauty and originality.

Having been a voice major, it is not surprising that
Sam Barber should have written a number of very beautiful songs. He also has written a large number of works
for the symphony orchestra, string orchestra, chamber
orchestra, for the ballet, and for voice and orchestra. He
has written music for the piano, a concerto for violoncello
and orchestra, and two operas — *Vanessa*, an opera in
four acts, and *A Hand of Bridge*, a short opera in one
act. The text for both of these operas was written by
his good friend and colleague, Gian-Carlo Menotti.

In 1943 Mr. Barber was inducted into the Army, where
he was given the assignment of loading and unloading
pianos and other musical instruments as they were moved
from one army camp to the next. The job was a boring
one so it is easy to understand why Mr. Barber was so
pleased to be transferred to the Air Force where he was
given time and encouragement to compose.

It was while he was in the service that he wrote the
"Commando March," which had its first performance by
the Army Air Force Band. His Second Symphony, commissioned by, and dedicated to the Army Air Force, was
first performed in 1944 by the Boston Symphony Orchestra.

Upon his release from military service, Mr. Barber returned to "Capricorn," a very large comfortable house, in
Mount Kisco, New York, which he shares with his composer friend Gian-Carlo Menotti. The years that followed
were some of the composer's most productive. His ballet

Medea, "Prayers of Kierkegaard" — for mixed chorus, soprano solo, and orchestra — a piano sonata, and his *Concerto for Violoncello and Orchestra* were written during this period. It was also at Capricorn that most of Mr. Barber's works after Opus 19 were written, including his opera *Vanessa*, which won for him the Pulitzer Prize in Music in 1958.

From his earliest childhood, Mr. Barber was rather shy. When alone with his family, he was affectionate and happy, especially with his sister Sara. But when visitors came to the house, he became quiet and retiring, and often disappeared to stay in his room. Most of his friends today still find him shy, but they are quick to admit to his delightful sense of humor.

Mr. Barber works slowly and, once an idea for a composition has entered his mind, becomes moody and disinterested in anything else until he has it written to his satisfaction. He often skips meals so as not to stop work. While he's working friends tend to leave him alone, but once he has finished they return again to his cheerful and pleasant company.

Of himself, Mr. Barber says, "I am the most unmechanical person in the world," and it appears that he is pretty close to being right. It takes him hours to wrap and tie a package which even then invariably must be done over again. He is never quite sure how to stop or start the phonograph or the tape recorder. Friends also say that he was undoubtedly the only soldier in the United States

Army who could not take his gun apart and put it together again. He enjoys good food, but cannot cook even an egg for himself.

Mr. Barber, who has often appeared as accompanist to his own songs, and as a pianist in recitals, no longer finds the time to make public appearances as a performer. He is president of the American Academy in Rome and has a heavy schedule of lecturing and meeting with and advising young composers. This, added to the time needed for his own composing, keeps him very busy indeed. He has few hobbies outside of reading, walking in the woods, mountain climbing, and collecting paintings by unknown artists.

The name of Sam Barber is probably the most respected name in American music and as such appears often on concert programs all over the world.

Leonard Bernstein

born in Lawrence, Massachusetts, August 25, 1918

At an age when most young musicians are still studying, Leonard Bernstein had reached the top of the musical profession, not only in one, but in three different fields of music. By the time he was twenty-five years old, he was recognized as a composer, a pianist, and a conductor. When asked how he could accomplish so much in so short a time, his reply was "Mostly luck." However, those who know Mr. Bernstein realize that none of these things could have been accomplished were he not one of the most talented musicians of the day.

Often when we read about great musicians, we find that they started music lessons at a very early age, and that many of them played or even composed music before they were ten years old. This is not true in Mr. Bernstein's case. The Bernstein family did not even have a piano in their home until Leonard was ten. Then an aunt, feeling her own house overcrowded, sent some furniture, that included a piano, to the Bernstein home.

Leonard, or "Lenny," as he is called by everyone who knows him, took his place at the piano, and it was hard to pull him away from it. After a month of his begging for lessons, the family found a teacher, and he was permitted to study.

No one in the family ever thought that Lenny would want to continue studying, or that he would want to earn his living as a musician. His father was in the cosmetics business and expected that his son would join him, but the boy had other ideas. Leonard Bernstein knew, shortly after he entered high school, that his chosen profession would be music.

After graduating from high school, Lenny became a student at Harvard University where as a music major he studied composition with Walter Piston and Edward Burlingame Hill, and piano with Heinrich Gebhard. It was at Harvard that he wrote his first serious music, a score for a play, *The Birds*. At the play performances he also conducted the student orchestra and showed unusual ability as a conductor. This presented a difficult problem: Since he was also a brilliant pianist, should he be a pianist, composer, or conductor?

In 1939, Mr. Bernstein graduated from Harvard and was advised to study conducting. In the fall of that year he became a student at the Curtis Institute of Music in Philadelphia. Fritz Reiner, who taught conducting there, was very pleased with his new pupil, but so were his teachers for piano and composition.

During the summer of 1941, Leonard Bernstein studied conducting at the Berkshire Music Festival in Massachusetts. Serge Koussevitzky, the conductor of the Boston Symphony Orchestra, was so pleased with him that he asked him to be his assistant the following summer. Only a year later Artur Rodzinski, conductor of the New York

Philharmonic Symphony, invited young Bernstein to become his assistant there, an almost unheard-of honor for anyone so young.

But Mr. Bernstein was not too young to prove himself. When Bruno Walter, who was to be guest conductor of the orchestra, became ill, Mr. Bernstein stepped in and conducted the concert. The program was broadcast nation-wide and was most successful. It immediately established Leonard Bernstein as a first-rate conductor.

Though most of us know Mr. Bernstein as a pianist and conductor, and have watched him conduct the New York Philharmonic on television, we also know him as a composer. He has written two symphonies and many ballets, which have been danced by the great ballet companies of the world. His concertos and sonatas have been performed by the outstanding musicians of our time, but his popular musicals, which have been produced on Broadway, have reached millions of people who might not know his other concert works.

Those who enjoy Leonard Bernstein's *West Side Story*, *Wonderful Town*, *Candide*, or *Fancy Free*, might also enjoy his serious works, such as his first symphony *Jeremiah* — which he started when he was twenty-four years old — or his second symphony, which he calls *The Age of Anxiety*.

Unlike many other composers, Mr. Bernstein feels that a composer does not have to restrict himself to writing only serious music. He has written music for everybody: four musical comedies, two symphonies, a violin serenade, two song cycles, a short opera, a clarinet sonata, two ballets, two piano suites, a motion picture score, incidental music for a play, and a long jazz composition called "Prelude, Fugue, and Riffs." He is as much at home with popular music and jazz as he is with his symphony orchestra and the music he conducts at Carnegie Hall. His music is alive, sincere, and it has something to give to the listener, whether it is played by a jazz band, sung on a Broadway stage, or played by one of our great symphony orchestras in a concert hall.

Mr. Bernstein has conducted most of the major orchestras in America and in Europe. He was the first American invited to conduct at the La Scala Opera. As conductor of the New York Philharmonic Symphony Orchestra, he has brought music to millions by means of television. He has also been a good-will cultural ambassador for the United States by taking the New York Philharmonic to Europe, Asia, and South America.

In the beginning, Mr. Bernstein never used a stick or baton to conduct. His friends wondered whether he did it in order to conserve energy or to appear more dignified. Most of the time he became so wrapped up in the music that he forgot the baton.

Mr. Bernstein is as great a delight to his musicians as he is to his audiences. Both at rehearsals and at concerts he sings every note of the music, at times at the top of his voice. It is not unusual for him to have little voice left at the end of a day of a rehearsal and concert.

It is difficult to do justice to Mr. Bernstein by describing him and his accomplishments. He was an excellent student in high school and at college. As a composer and conductor, his work is imaginative and he can communicate the emotions he experiences to his audiences. Everything he does seems easy to him. He can learn several scores, in preparation for a concert, in a matter of days. Though he often says that he does not practice, his piano playing is of the highest caliber. He speaks German, French, Italian, and Hebrew fluently. He is capable of composing while riding in a taxi, or plane, or in a railroad station or hotel lobby. He is a fascinating speaker, but also a good listener. He has an overwhelming loyalty to his family and friends and, although a world figure himself, he always has time for young people — to listen to their problems and to advise and help them.

There are many demands on Leonard Bernstein's time and often he is overburdened. But when it is suggested that he drop some of the things he is doing he says, "I don't want to give in and settle for some specialty . . . it would bore me to death. I want to conduct, I want to play the piano, I want to write music for Broadway and Hollywood, I want to write symphonic music, I want to keep on trying to be in the full sense of that wonderful word, a musician. I want to teach, I want to write books and poetry, and I think I can, and still do justice to them all."

Mr. Bernstein, his wife, the former actress Felicia Montealegre, and their three children, Jamie, Alexander Serge, and a baby sister, live in a large penthouse apartment on Park Avenue. He finds time to play with the children and entertain his many friends. He likes to stay up late, and loves to spend time on crossword puzzles, often hiding them in the scores that are always before him.

To audiences who have watched Mr. Bernstein conduct, he seems much taller than his five feet eight and one-half inches. His head is often spoken of as "his lion head" because of the "mane" of graying hair. He chooses his clothes very carefully, and is especially fond of Italian-made shoes. He also loves bright red sweaters which he often wears at rehearsals.

Mr. Bernstein has an idea of his worth, yet is not overwhelmed by it. He dislikes criticism, and very often disagrees with his critics, but he is charming and gracious to the people who come to speak to him backstage after a concert.

Aaron Copland

born in Brooklyn, New York, November 14, 1900

AARON COPLAND was born and reared in an old Irish-Italian section of Brooklyn, New York. His was not a musical family. By the time he wanted to learn to play the piano, his parents had spent so much money, without results, on piano lessons for the four older Copland children, that they felt it would be a waste of money to give lessons to their youngest child. Finally, however, the boy convinced them and his musical career was started.

For several years Aaron studied piano, but he found that he was really more interested in writing music. After two more years of piano study and a correspondence course in theory and harmony, he became a pupil of Rubin Goldmark, an excellent musician and teacher.

The first composition Mr. Copland wrote was a piece for piano which he called "Cat and the Mouse." The work did not impress his teacher — it was different, too modern! Mr. Goldmark was certain that his pupil would never become a composer. (Several years later, while studying in Paris, Mr. Copland played his piece and sold it to a publisher for twenty-five dollars.)

Aaron Copland went to France when he was twenty-one years old. There he studied composition for three years with Nadia Boulanger. Also he produced several motets

for unaccompanied voices, a song for soprano with accompaniment of flute and clarinet, and a one-act ballet for orchestra called "Grohg."

In 1924 he returned to America with his completed works and a big assignment. Miss Boulanger, who was not only an outstanding teacher of composition but a fine organist as well, was engaged to appear the following year as a soloist with the New York Philharmonic Symphony Orchestra. She asked her pupil Aaron to write for the occasion a symphony for organ and orchestra.

This work, *Symphony for Organ and Orchestra*, the first of Mr. Copland's work to be performed in the United States, was first played by the New York Philharmonic. Walter Damrosch conducted and Miss Boulanger was the soloist. The New York audience found the composition a little "too modern" but it received most enthusiastic praise when it was later performed in Boston by the Boston Symphony Orchestra under the direction of Koussevitzky.

During his years of study in Europe, Mr. Copland's family helped him financially but, on his return, it was expected that he would earn money from his music. Thus he was faced with the problem of making a living and it was a hard task to face. America was not yet ready for the music of its young composers.

A job as a pianist in a hotel trio tided Mr. Copland over the summer. In the fall of 1924, he opened a studio and announced that "the teaching services of Aaron Copland, recently returned from Europe, are available." The venture met with little success — not a single pupil came for lessons! Things looked very bleak indeed, until a Guggenheim Fellowship made it possible for the composer to work, free of money worries for several years.

Financial problems were not the only ones that plagued the young composer. He often had trouble with neighbors who did not appreciate the fact that he did his best composing late at night when everyone was asleep! The problem was a real one for Mr. Copland, until he finally found complete freedom at the MacDowell Colony. There, where he could work without any restrictions, some of his very finest music was composed.

Mr. Copland has a long list of compositions to his credit. He has written operas, ballets, chamber music, concertos, and symphonies, and one can hear his works played throughout the world. He also has been an inspiration and a great help to many other American composers, for he has worked hard to get their works performed and to give them greater financial security.

Like a true artist, Aaron Copland's music expresses the life, the times, and the pulse of the country in which he lives. Many of his works have been selected to represent the United States at international music festivals. His style is definitely his own, but his music sounds undoubtedly American. He, more than most composers, catches the feeling of American folklore. At times he actually makes use of folk tunes in his music, and at times he writes colorful melodies which sound like folk tunes.

Tall, straight, vigorous, and youthful looking, despite his

almost completely white hair, Mr. Copland's interests are many and varied. His wide circle of friends represents many different professions in the business world as well as the arts. His love for modern dance and ballet has brought him into close contact with some of the great dancers of our time and he has written some of his best works for them.

Rodeo was written for the famous dancer-choreographer Agnes de Mille, who supplied the story. In this work, Mr. Copland paints a fine picture of the life of cowboys in our western states and actually uses several western folk tunes. *El Salón México* was written for orchestra and is based on old Mexican folk tunes he discovered on his first trip to Mexico. *Billy the Kid* was written for Ballet Caravan. Here Mr. Copland uses simple cowboy songs as basic melodies. His ballet *Appalachian Spring* was written for the dancer Martha Graham. This work contains some of the folk tunes of the Appalachian region and won for him the Pulitzer Prize in Music.

With his music, Mr. Copland wants to reach the people, all the people who hear his music. He wants even amateur groups to be able to play his compositions, and he wrote his short opera "The Second Hurricane" especially for high-school singers. His charming piano piece, "Down a Country Lane," was written for young piano pupils. Of it Mr. Copland says, "This composition is a bigger challenge than it first looks, and even a third-year student will have to practice before trying it in public." This piano piece is still another indication of the composer's concern and interest in the people, young and old, whom he is constantly trying to reach.

Mr. Copland lives in Peekskill, New York, in a large house overlooking the Hudson. Despite a very busy schedule of composing, conducting, writing, lecturing, and teaching, he finds time to examine the scores of the young composers who seek his help and advice.

Aaron Copland's best time for composing is still late at night. He often starts at dinner-time and works all night in order to complete something he has started. His pockets are full of scraps of paper on which he has written down ideas, rhythms, and tunes. He may often be seen at concerts, for he likes "live" music. He says, "Recordings are really for people who live in Timbuktu."

In *Music Today*, Dr. Carleton Sprague Smith, musicologist, wrote: "Aaron Copland is without question North America's leading composer. He has a flavour which is at once personal and American . . . He can be grand, solemn or gay — bleak or 'juicy.' As a teacher, public lecturer, author, pianist and conductor, Copland has had the greatest influence of any composer now active in the United States."

Henry Dixon Cowell

born in Menlo Park, California, on March 11, 1897

Even as a child, Henry Dixon Cowell gave every indication that he was an individualist, that he knew what he wanted and how to pursue it, and that he had the determination and temperament to become the musician he is today. Because of his frail constitution during childhood, and his English-Irish parents' theory that formal education was not a necessity for everyone, Henry did not attend school as did other children of his age. When the boy was five years old he started to play the violin, and two years later was attempting Mozart and Beethoven sonatas in recital.

The following year, his health had become so much worse that he gave his violin away and devoted his time to the development of "more perfect hearing" in his mind. He had decided to become a composer and, since there was no piano in the Cowell household, Henry practiced "mentally" each day on an imaginary piano keyboard. Meanwhile he earned money by growing and selling unusual plants and, after several years of saving, he was able to buy an old piano which became the very joy of his existence.

By this time he was fourteen years old and, since he was not going to school, he spent all of his time at the piano.

He began to experiment and to develop some theories about tone. He discovered what he called "tone clusters," a combination of notes that form chords very different from the ones our ears are accustomed to. Instead of being built on thirds and fifths, his "tone clusters" consisted of chords formed by striking the piano keys with the whole hand, fist, or elbow. The idea was not entirely original, as jazz pianists and some other composers had used the technique, but Cowell's naming the chords "tone clusters" attracted much attention.

In 1912, when only fifteen years old, Henry Cowell made his first public appearance in a program of his own music at the San Francisco Music Club. The audience was both surprised and shocked by the sounds and combinations of sounds they had never heard from a piano before.

Cowell applied his knowledge of the violin to the piano and plucked the piano strings by hand as one would play the pizzicato on the violin or any other string instrument. His compositions called for the pianist to use the palm of his hand, the closed fist, the elbow, or the forearm on the piano keys. This was a most unusual way to use the piano but the results were most interesting and certainly unique.

At seventeen, with about one hundred compositions to his credit, Henry Cowell realized that he had very little formal music training and felt the need for it. A number of his friends made it possible for him to study at the University of California. Since he had never attended high school, he could not be given college credit for his courses, but he did remain at the university for three and one-half years. At the end of that time he was given an assistant-ship in the music department.

During the First World War, Cowell enlisted in the United States Army and conducted an army band in Allentown, Pennsylvania. When he was discharged, he continued his music studies for two more years at the Institute of Applied Music in New York City.

It was an important step for the composer. He had the opportunity there to meet other musicians and discuss his music. He was able to prove that his "unconventional" use of the piano produced excellent effects. The results were a better understanding and appreciation of Cowell's music.

Within the ten-year period from 1923–1933, the composer made a tour of the United States and five tours of Europe, playing programs consisting entirely of his own works. Pianists began to show interest in his compositions, and even some of the music critics who had not been too kind in their reviews began to see some good qualities in his music. In 1928, Mr. Cowell received an official invitation to perform in Russia. His music was so well received that two of his works, "Tiger" and "Reel," were the first works by an American composer to be published in Soviet Russia.

Arthur Schnabel, the well-known pianist, became so fascinated with Cowell's music that he not only learned and played some of his piano works, but also arranged a concert for the composer in Berlin, Germany. The famous Hungarian composer-pianist Béla Bartók also became interested in Henry Cowell and arranged a concert for him in Paris so that the French would be sure to hear the music of this strange, unusual American composer. By 1940, more than two hundred and fifty pianists were performing Cowell's piano works in Europe and America.

It is rather difficult to weigh or even thoroughly discuss Henry Cowell's contribution to American music. Primarily he wanted greater freedom from rigid forms of composition. He wanted to explore all possibilities for writing music which was different in style and pattern from that of the old masters. Audiences and musicians have not always agreed with his ideas or theories, but everyone who knows his music will readily agree that the composer has shown courage, originality, and ingenuity, and that he is a gifted musician.

Mr. Cowell is recognized not only as a composer, but as a teacher, lecturer, editor, experimenter, pianist, and author. His contributions in the field of music are varied and wide. He is the author of *New Musical Resources*, and one-time editor of, and contributor to *American Composers on American Music*. His text *The Nature of Melody* has proven very useful to many young composers. He is also the founder of a non-profit organization which issues a quarterly periodical devoted to publishing the scores of experimental new music.

Today Mr. Cowell is known and remembered not only for his "tone clusters," but for the large number of his compositions that are performed in this country, in Europe, and in South America. He has written music for orchestra and chamber orchestra, band music, chamber music, and choral works. He has also written music for films and ballet.

Henry Cowell writes easily and quickly. He often outlines a whole work at one sitting and has been known to say that he would much rather begin on a new composition than work on one he had started. He often relies on folk tunes of all nations for ideas and inspiration. Some of his more recent works are his settings from the "Dead Sea Scrolls" for chorus and orchestra, his *Symphony No. 12* and his "Variations for Orchestra."

The combinations of instruments which Mr. Cowell uses in many of his works are as unusual as some of the titles he has given them. For his ballet *The Building of Banba* he requires five solo singers, a chorus, and fourteen orchestral instruments. In his choral work "Fire and Ice" his score calls for two tenors, baritone, bass, and orchestra or band. His "Rhythmicana" calls for his invention the "rhythmicon" and an orchestra. One of his chamber music works is called "Seven Paragraphs," and a work for orchestra has the name "Ongaku."

The following quotation from an article "Henry Cowell, Musician and Citizen" which appeared in *Etude* Magazine most aptly explains our musical debt to Henry Cowell.

> The debt of American music to Henry Cowell is large and substantial. He has had a major role in freeing our music from the slavish imitation of European models . . . He is largely responsible for the acceptance today of experimental tendencies

... As a creative musician, he has done all in his power to bring American music of age, and his hand has been a powerful one in shaping our musical culture . . .

Paul Creston

born in New York City on October 10, 1906

MORE THAN almost anyone else, Paul Creston has proven that "where there is a will there is a way," for he became one of our foremost composers despite great hardships and deprivation.

At birth Paul Creston was named Joseph Guttoveggio by his Italian parents. His father was a house painter and, during the years that Paul and his brother were growing up, he was often out of work and the family was very poor. Yet when Paul's brother wanted to play the violin, a violin was obtained for him. But to everyone's surprise Paul did most of the practicing on it.

When Paul was eight years old he very much wanted a piano and the family resources were pooled. One was purchased for ten dollars, and further family sacrifices were made for piano lessons. His piano teacher taught not only piano but all other instruments as well. Unfortunately, though, he could not play any of them himself, and much of Paul's precious money and time were wasted for a period of six years. During these years, however, Paul was learning a great deal by reading books on music fundamentals and on the piano.

When Paul was fourteen years old, he was convinced that what he needed most was more organized music

study. He then became a pupil of Aldo Randegger and Gaston Dethier, and studied organ with the famous organist of St. Patrick's Cathedral in New York, Pietro Yon. Unfortunately, after a rather short period of time, he had to discontinue these studies because he could not afford to pay for his lessons. He also had to drop out of high school before he had finished his third year and go to work to help support himself and his family.

Paul Creston took any job he could find, but he never stopped studying and working on his music. He always spent at least two hours practicing in the morning, before going to his job at nine. After work he returned to his music, working late into the night. He often said, "If Edison could get along on four hours sleep, I can too."

Thus determination and hard work made Paul Creston the composer he is today. Self-taught and self-educated, he has had a very successful career as a lecturer, pianist, organist, conductor, and composer.

His first composition, a set of "Five Dances for Piano," was written in 1932. Since then he has written many works in many different forms for a variety of instruments. His First Symphony, completed in 1940, was performed by the Philadelphia Orchestra, and was selected by the Music Critics Circle as the outstanding new American work of that year. In 1945 his Second Symphony was introduced by the New York Philharmonic.

Another of his major works "Chant of 1942" was inspired by the grave events of the war. His "Frontiers," commissioned by conductor Andre Kostelanetz, was inspired by American history and the migration to the West. "Pastorale," "Tarantella," and "Prelude and Dance" for orchestra, and his Third Symphony written in 1950, are great favorites with audiences.

Mr. Creston has always been interested in unusual instruments, especially those for which very little music has been written. His *Concerto for Marimba and Orchestra* was first performed at the Yaddo Contemporary Music Festival in 1940. He was also interested in elevating the saxophone to the status of a solo instrument and wrote a suite, a sonata, and a concerto featuring it. In 1958 Mr. Creston wrote *Concerto for Accordion and Orchestra*.

Beside orchestral works Mr. Creston has written chamber music, music for bands, songs, choral works, and many compositions for the piano. His music is rich, sincere, full of warmth and color. Because he does not especially like titles that are too descriptive, he invariably supplies notes about his music and has been very fortunate in having most of his works published. Though of Italian ancestry, he is often spoken of as the "solid contemporary composer with the typically American flavor."

Paul Creston and his family live in White Plains, New York. He is very mechanical and does most of the work necessary to keep his home in excellent condition. He is extremely orderly and organizes his time so that not one minute is wasted.

To facilitate the writing of his music, he has invented several systems of musical shorthand. He composes in the morning when he is fresh and rested. His wife, Louise, has her sons, neighbors and visitors well trained — no interruptions in the morning when Mr. Creston is working!

The Crestons live very simply. Paul Creston hates parties and large crowds. Tennis and swimming are his favorite sports and he has passed these interests on to his sons. He is an excellent photographer and loves to work puzzles. Also he is an avid reader and has studied hypnotism, astrology and yoga.

Mr. Creston has great faith in his own works and when a conductor requests him to make some change, he firmly but politely informs him that he likes his music the way it was written. He would rather not have the work performed if a change must be made.

Mr. Creston has the same attitude toward criticism of his works. Uncomplimentary comments do not upset him. He feels that it is unfair for critics to judge a work the first time it is played, for a proper judgment can be made only after a number of performances.

Paul Creston has a very prominent place among American composers. He has received many honors, commissions, and fellowships. His contribution to music is impressive and covers a wide range. His works are performed regularly in the United States and in Europe and many of them have been recorded. He also is in demand as pianist, organist, conductor, teacher, and lecturer.

John Rosenfeld of the *Dallas Morning News* in speaking of Paul Creston says, "What has impressed us about Creston is not only his individuality but also the broadness and freshness of viewpoint . . . His is music that combines the Italian gift for song or lyricism with an arresting self-taught use of all that has been accomplished by expansive orchestral study."

Paul Creston may well be singled out as an American success story!

Norman Dello Joio

born in New York City, January 24, 1913

NORMAN DELLO JOIO comes from a long line of professional musicians. His father, who was born in Naples, was a church organist in New York City, and gave his son his first lessons on the piano and organ. When he was fifteen years old, Pietro Yon, Norman's godfather and well-known organist of St. Patrick's Cathedral in New York, became his teacher. Later he continued his studies at the Juilliard School of Music with Gaston Dethier and Bernard Wagenaar, then at Yale University with Paul Hindemith.

Long before he was twenty years old, Norman Dello Joio was able to assist his father at the church organ. It proved very good experience for he later had numerous jobs as choir director and organist. Mr. Dello Joio was also for a time musical director of the well-known dance group Dance Players. And he toured with his own jazz band which he organized and conducted. Later he became teacher of composition at Sarah Lawrence College in Bronxville, New York.

Although the composer has said "I never expected to be anything but a musician," he spent considerable time in his teens playing baseball. The game fascinated him and he showed such amazing skill at it that he was offered a contract to become professional. He was extremely

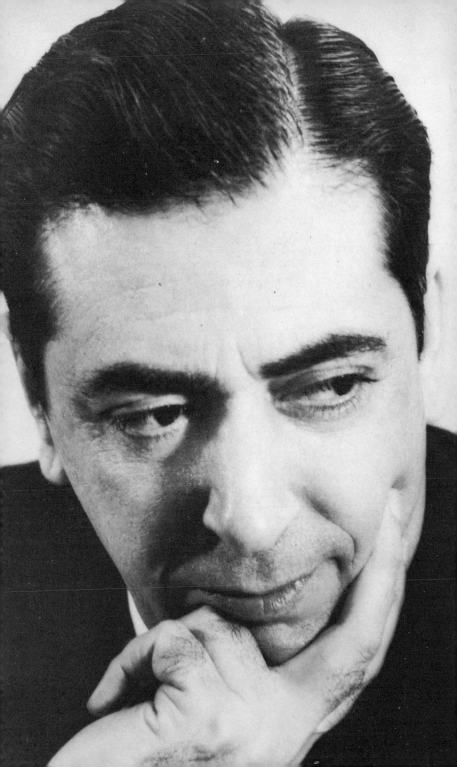

pleased by the offer but refused it. Never for a moment has he regretted the decision.

It was not until Mr. Dello Joio went to the Juilliard School of Music that he started to compose. The first composition to bring him recognition was a "Piano Trio" which won him the Elizabeth Sprague Coolidge Prize in 1939. Since then Mr. Dello Joio has received many awards and prizes. Among them are the Town Hall Composition Award for his "Magnificat" in 1941, Guggenheim Fellowships in 1943 and 1944, and the New York Music Critics Circle Award for his "Variations, Chaconne, and Finale" in 1948. In 1957 his orchestral work "Meditations on Ecclesiastes" won the Pulitzer Prize, and in 1960 he was again awarded the New York Music Critics Circle Award.

Mr. Dello Joio is hailed as one of the foremost contemporary composers on the American scene. His list of works is long and covers a wide range from songs and piano solos to chamber music, symphonic works, cantatas, operas, and ballets. He also has written background music for some impressive television shows, and incidental music for the stage.

His music shows a fine technical mastery and a directness of expression with strong emotional appeal. It is often described as "exhilarating" and "dramatic" and, though unmistakably modern, "it is rich in fluent, spontaneous sounding melodic contours."

The choral work, *Song of Affirmation; Cantata for Chorus, Navator, Soprano and Full Orchestra*, was written

to the text of "Western Star" by the poet Stephen Vincent
Benét. It was commissioned by conductor Robert Shaw
for the Collegiate Chorale and is a powerful, convincing
work, both lyrical and sensitive.

Of the composer's three ballets, *Prairie* and *Duke of
Sacramento* were commissioned by Eugene Loring. They
were written for Loring's dancers whom Mr. Dello Joio
directed for a time. *On Stage* was commissioned by the
Ballet Theater and has become a major part of ballet
repertoire.

Perhaps one of the composer's most dramatic works is
his opera *Trial at Rouen*, which is the story of Joan of
Arc. It was presented on television and was immediately
acclaimed a work of tremendous proportion. In it Mr.
Dello Joio shows his keen sense of the dramatic and his
great gift for melody.

Another opera, *Blood Moon*, was introduced in San
Francisco by the San Francisco Opera Company and was
welcomed and praised by audiences and critics. Dello
Joio's style leans toward the popular, and his directness
of thought and gift for the melodic touch the people who
hear his music.

Married to a former ballerina, Norman Dello Joio lives
in New York City, where he divides his time between
composing and teaching composition at the David Mannes
School of Music. Most of his works have been published,
many are recorded, and he enjoys wide recognition. In
1961 he was elected to membership in the National Institute of Arts and Letters.

The *New York Times* well described the music of Norman Dello Joio . . . "The composer writes with spirit and grace. He does not seem to be weighted down by the consciousness that he must be significant at all costs, and, oddly enough, the music stays with you longer because it is unpretentious."

Lukas Foss

born in Berlin, Germany, August 15, 1922

ALTHOUGH BORN IN GERMANY, Lukas Foss is considered an American composer, because he came to the United States when he was fifteen years old and because almost all of his compositions were written in this country.

From the time that he was a very young boy, Lukas Foss showed great musical ability. His first composition was written when he was seven years old, and by the time he was in his mid-teens he was known as an excellent pianist. Like most youthful musicians, young Lukas was a great admirer of the classical composers — he was especially devoted to the works of Bach and Haydn — and thus his early works were written in the classic style. When he was fourteen years old, however, he became acquainted with the music of another German-born composer Paul Hindemith, who lived in the United States. Deeply impressed, Lukas's style of writing soon changed from the purely classical to the more modern style of Hindemith.

Upon leaving Germany, Foss studied piano and composition at the Paris Conservatory for two years. Then, when he came to the United States in 1937, he became a student at the Curtis Institute of Music in Philadelphia. There he studied composition, conducting, and piano.

Lukas spent several summers at Tanglewood, Massachu-

setts, where he studied conducting with Serge Koussevitzky, the late conductor of the Boston Symphony Orchestra. He also studied composition there with Paul Hindemith, whom he had long admired and who continued to have a great influence on him. In 1944 he was appointed official pianist of the Boston Symphony Orchestra, a post he held for six years.

Lukas Foss is an intensely interesting personality. He is energetic and convincing, and he has a strong sense of independence. Despite his considerable gifts as a pianist and conductor, he has not allowed them to interfere with his work as a composer.

In 1942 he was commissioned by the Theater Guild to write incidental music to Shakespeare's *The Tempest*. This music won him a Pulitzer Traveling Scholarship. During the same year, his "Allegro Concertante" was introduced in Philadelphia and New York with the composer conducting. These works were well received but it was his cantata *The Prairie*, commissioned by Robert Shaw and the Collegiate Chorale, that brought him to the forefront of the music world and established him as a major modern composer. In this work, Mr. Foss used as his text a poem by Carl Sandburg. It is amazing that *The Prairie* should have been written by a young man, born in Germany, who had been in this country only about six or seven years. The composition, American to the core, presents a picture of the vastness of our country and the vigor and strength of the people who settled it and made it the great nation it is. *The Prairie* received the Music Critic's Circle

Award as the most important choral work of the season.

Lukas Foss has written a large number of compositions which are performed all over the world. Besides *The Prairie*, he has written *Concerto for Piano and Orchestra*, *Symphony in G*, and "Ode" dedicated to those who did not return, and introduced by the New York Philharmonic with George Szell conducting. The *Symphony of Chorales* was commissioned by the Koussevitzky Music Foundation and composed at the request of the Friends of Albert Schweitzer in Boston. His ballet *The Gift of the Magi*, based on the O. Henry story by the same name, was performed by the Ballet Theater. His *Song of Songs*, a *Biblical Solo Cantata*, commissioned by the League of Composers, was introduced in Boston by the late Serge Koussevitzky and the Boston Symphony Orchestra. The conductor was so impressed with the work that he played it eight times in nine days, in order that as many people as possible could hear it.

Mr. Foss's works also include chamber music, piano solos, and operas. His three-act opera, *Griffelkin*, based on a German fairy tale, was commissioned by the National Broadcasting Company, and it was produced on television in November of 1956. Another of his operas, *Introductions and Goodbyes* was written to the libretto of composer Gian-Carlo Menotti and was commissioned by the Festival of Two Worlds in Spoleto, Italy. It was given its premiere in concert form, in May, 1960, by Leonard Bernstein and the New York Philharmonic. One month later it had its first stage production at Spoleto.

Since 1953 Mr. Foss has held a professorship in composition at the University of California in Los Angeles, where he is influential in guiding and helping many young people who are studying to become composers.

One of Mr. Foss's works, "Time Cycle for Soprano and Orchestra," was commissioned by soprano Adele Addison and is considered one of his finest and most beautiful compositions. Leonard Bernstein and the New York Philharmonic introduced the work in October of 1960 with Miss Addison as soloist.

Mr. Foss is now a well-established composer whose music appears on concert programs throughout the world. He has received many prizes, awards, and fellowships, and his guest appearances as piano soloist and as conductor with many major American orchestras have earned for him as well a reputation as a fine performer.

Stephen Collins Foster

---

*born in Pittsburgh, Pennsylvania, July 4, 1826,
died in New York City, January 13, 1864*

THERE IS HARDLY a man, woman, or child in the country who does not know some of the music of Stephen Collins Foster. His music is sung in the schoolroom, in the concert hall, and hummed by the housewife doing her chores at home. Among the approximately 180 songs written by this much-loved American composer, there is something soothing and beautiful to fit every need and every mood.

Stephen Collins Foster, the youngest of nine children, was born in Pittsburgh, Pennsylvania, on the Fourth of July, 1826. His parents, who were of Scotch-Irish ancestry, were well educated and expected that their youngest son would one day become a fine gentleman. The Foster family was a happy one and the large white house in which they lived rang with laughter and music.

As the baby of the family, Stephen received a great deal of attention and love. His sisters were all rather musical and spent much time around the piano singing to the accompaniment of the guitar. By the time he was two, Stephen put the guitar — which he called his little piano — on the floor and played tunes by plucking the strings. His sisters were pleased and excited by their brother's

ability and interest in music, but his older brothers paid no attention to it. Music was not for boys!

Perhaps the most musical members of the Foster household were Live and Tom, the "bounded" girl and boy who were servants to the Fosters. Young Stephen followed them around as they worked at their chores and listened to their songs.

Live and Tom were always singing and often Stephen joined them. He was allowed to go to the Negro church with them and sat fascinated as he listened to the singing. There was something about the songs of the Negroes that appealed to him and Stephen was forever playing them on the piano.

Stephen's teacher Henry Kleber — the only one he had ever had — did not altogether approve of, or appreciate Stephen's feelings for Negro music but, fortunately, Mr. Kleber had little influence on his young pupil. Before very long the two parted company and Stephen was on his own.

Stephen finally convinced even his brothers that it was fun to be able to sing Negro spirituals and together they put on many minstrel shows. The boys blackened their faces, sang, and danced, and, though all of them were good, it was Stephen who could best imitate the Negro dialect and dances. He often thought he would like to become an entertainer and earn his living as one, but his older brothers greatly disapproved. They told him firmly that it was expected that he receive a good education and that he earn his livelihood doing "man's work."

When Stephen was ten years old, the family met with

financial difficulties. Business was poor and his father could no longer support his large family and the white house in which they had all been so happy. The family moved to several different towns in search of work for Stephen's father and for a brief time lived with one of the boy's uncles in Poland, Ohio. It was this uncle who was so impressed with his young nephew's musical ability that he said Stephen would be "a famous man, if he lived long enough."

At the age of thirteen, Stephen became a student at the Academy in Tioga Point, Pennsylvania. Though he was unhappy and had a profound dislike for the school, nevertheless he worked hard at his lessons and there wrote his first composition. It was the "Tioga Waltz," a work for three flutes that he and two of his classmates performed in the school auditorium.

The following year, after passing all of his examinations at the Academy, Stephen Foster enrolled as a student at Jefferson College in Canonsburg, Pennsylvania. Before the first week was over though, he knew that he didn't really wish to study there, so he promptly left the college. Thus, at the age of fourteen, his schooling was over, and Stephen began to devote all of his time to composing. His "Open thy Lattice Love," was published when he was sixteen years old.

Meanwhile the Foster family had moved back to Pittsburgh where Stephen and his brother, whom he called "Mit," belonged to a singing club that rehearsed most often at the Foster home. Whenever the group was in doubt about some new selection to sing, Stephen offered to write a song. It was for his club that he wrote the words and music for "Lou'siana Belle" which the boys sang in Negro dialect. Some weeks later he wrote "Old Uncle Ned," considered one of his finest compositions.

By the time Stephen was twenty years old, he had written and published a large number of songs, but had earned very little money as a result. His family was not impressed with his song-writing.

Finally brother Dunning, who was in business on the waterfront in Cincinnati, convinced him to work there as a bookkeeper. Stephen accepted the job and spent his days on a high stool, watching the Negro stevedores unloading bales of cotton, baskets of fruit, heavy sacks of sugar, and other goods. As he watched these strong-muscled men, he listened to the songs they always sang as they worked. At times, he forgot the books and figures in front of him as he swayed with the rhythmic music of mèn hard at work.

During Stephen Foster's first year in Cincinnati, his ever-popular "Oh! Susanna," was published. It was an immediate success; every minstrel in the country sang it, yet it earned very little money for Stephen. He became so discouraged that he began to give away his songs to friends or anyone else who wanted to sing them.

It was only after Stephen Foster learned that his publisher had earned ten thousand dollars from the sales of "Oh! Susanna," and "Old Uncle Ned," that he decided to give up the job that he had had for three years. He returned to his family in Pittsburgh and began to work full time on composition.

In 1850, at the age of twenty-four, Stephen Foster married Jane McDowell, the daughter of a Pittsburgh physician. He was extremely happy and wrote some of his best-loved songs during his early marriage years: "Old Folks at Home," "Massa's in the Cold, Cold Ground," and "Jeanie with the Light Brown Hair" — which he wrote especially for his wife Jane.

Within a period of five years, there were forty-two songs — forty-two good songs that were used by minstrels all over the country. But still they did not pay enough to the composer to enable him to take care of his wife and his baby daughter Marion. These were days of great disappointment and discouragement and Stephen decided to take his family to New York and try his luck there.

The move did not prove to be a good one. Things seemed to go from bad to worse. The family kept moving from one rooming house to the next, from one miserable place to another. There was often no money to pay the rent or to buy food. Stephen simply was not a good businessman.

Publishers and performers took advantage of him. One entertainer paid him fifteen dollars for "Old Folks at Home," not only for the privilege of singing it, but for the privilege of saying that he, not Foster, had written the song!

After a period of great discomfort, poverty, and unhappiness, Mrs. Foster and her child left New York. Stephen remained there, still hopeful that his songs would bring him enough income to take care of his family.

On the thirteenth of January, 1864, Stephen Foster died as a result of a fall in his rooming house. For several days after the fall he had remained in his room — too poor to call a doctor. When finally he was taken to the charity ward of Bellevue Hospital, it was too late to do anything to save him.

Stephen was only thirty-eight years old at the time of his death. His death certificate gave his occupation as "laborer"; his pockets contained thirty-eight cents, all he had left from a lifetime of song-writing.

In his brief lifetime, Stephen Foster wrote some two hundred works. Of these, about one hundred and eighty-eight are folk songs and ballads; many of them had words as well as the music written by Foster. They are simple songs, often very sad, but always full of feeling and beauty.

Today the world appreciates the music of Stephen Collins Foster. Few composers are as loved and as well known by as many people. Statues of him are to be found in schools, parks, and public places throughout the nation.

A most suitable tribute to the composer is found in the composer's birthplace in Pittsburgh, Pennsylvania. There, at the University of Pittsburgh, the Stephen Foster Memorial Association has collected many of the composer's original compositions and a wealth of material about his life. In 1941, Stephen Collins Foster was elected to the Hall of Fame, a great honor indeed. But the greatest tribute to the composer is the love and pride Americans feel in his simple words and touchingly beautiful melodies.

George Gershwin

born in Brooklyn, New York, September 25, 1898,
died in Hollywood, California, 1937

ANYONE WHO KNEW GEORGE GERSHWIN as a little boy would probably never have said that he would some day be one of America's best-known composers. Born in Brooklyn, he grew up on New York's East Side. The neighborhood was busy and overcrowded, and there young George became the roller-skating champion.

George did not take music lessons, nor did he go to concerts. There was no piano in the Gershwin home. He was much more interested in baseball, and besides, he and his friends believed that only girls and "sissies" studied music!

When he was about ten years old, George Gershwin first became aware of the beauty of music and was deeply touched by it. A pupil in the elementary school he attended played the violin in the school auditorium during a recess. George did not know that the young violinist Maxie Rosenzweig (who later became the well-known violinist Max Rosen), was playing Dvořák's "Humoresque" but, unashamed before his "hardhitting" friends, he just stood and listened. He had never before heard anything so delightful.

After school he waited to see Maxie, but Maxie had left for the day. George went to his home, and the two young

people became good friends. Though Max Rosen did not believe that Gershwin would ever become a musician, he influenced and helped him greatly.

When the Gershwins finally bought a piano, it was with the idea that quiet, studious Ira, George's older brother, was to take piano lessons. Ira, however, did not want piano lessons; he preferred to read. But the piano did not go to waste — George used it every free minute he had. When he was thirteen, he finally convinced his family that he ought to have lessons.

The several teachers with whom George first worked were not very helpful or inspiring. It was Charles Hambilzer who first opened the world of music to him. Hambilzer was a hard taskmaster who insisted on good piano technique and introduced his young pupil to the great classical masters, Bach, Beethoven, and Mozart. Even though he knew that his pupil was much more interested in "this modern stuff, jazz," he felt that the boy needed a sound background.

At sixteen George left the Commercial High School he was attending and took a job with Remick's, a publisher of popular music. He was a "song plugger," and it was his job to interest singers and actors in the music published by the firm. Very often, when the day's work was over, the pluggers would go to night clubs and play their firm's songs, always hoping to get more people to sing and buy their music.

At the end of two years, George left Remick's and accepted a job with the Harms publishing house. It was a good offer. He would receive thirty-five dollars a week and no specified hours to work, so he would have time for composing and studying. The head of Harms had confidence that George Gershwin would one day write great music.

It is interesting to note that up to this time, though George Gershwin already had written a number of songs, none were immediately successful. His first musical comedy *La, La, Lucille* was written when he was twenty-one. Soon after, however, he wrote "Swanee," a song which sold more than a million copies.

Some of Gershwin's most popular music followed. He wrote song hits, musical comedies, and Broadway musicals, including the score for *George White's Scandals*. He became very successful financially and enjoyed great popularity. People who never went to concerts knew the name of George Gershwin, and the policeman on the corner and the man on the street hummed his music.

George Gershwin, however, was not entirely satisfied with all his success. There was in him an urge, a restlessness, and a feeling that he had fallen short of his musical aim. He was forever studying and striving to write better music about the America he knew and loved, and about her people. It was as if he had a premonition of his early death and wanted to write music that would live long after he was gone. He didn't seem to realize that it was his music that brought new audiences to listen to the vibrant rhythms of jazz and gave them a new respect for it. With his *Rhapsody in Blue*, written for Paul Whiteman and performed at Aeolian Hall in New York City, jazz music suddenly became serious music and invaded the concert hall.

In 1925, Gershwin's *Concerto in F* for piano was performed in Carnegie Hall. Concert-goers who came to the hall out of curiosity about the "new jazz," were amazed at the freshness and beauty of the work.

Three years later, as a well-recognized composer, George Gershwin went to Paris for a much-needed vacation. He was fascinated by the atmosphere and people of Paris. He walked, watched, and listened to the city during the day and at night. The result was his famous "An American in Paris."

Perhaps Gershwin's greatest work was his folk opera *Porgy and Bess*. The opera, based on Negro life, is full of humor and pathos, and is in every way a "portrait of a race," beautifully and artistically done. Gershwin worked on it in New York and in the South for almost a full year and when it was finished he said that, of all his works, *Porgy and Bess* was his very favorite.

Musical and financial success made it possible for George to move his parents to a good neighborhood and to give his mother the things that she could never afford when her children were small. Of her, George often said, "My Mom is just the kind about whom 'Mommy' songs are written." His mother was always interested in George's latest work and was proud of him and her other son, Ira. Ira had written the text for *Porgy and Bess* and for many of his brother's other works.

George loved gadgets and his mother had every imaginable invention that might make housekeeping easier and more comfortable. George also had some inventions of his own. He had built a special desk so that he could write while composing at the piano. The desk had wheels and one side was hollowed out to fit his middle. Thus he had ample and comfortable working space. The composer usually worked at night — often working through half the night, while the house and city streets were quiet — and therefore slept mornings.

The Gershwins had many friends and there was hardly an evening when people did not "drop in." Mrs. Gershwin was never happier than when she was serving special delicacies to her sons and their friends. These evenings were always filled with music and it was not at all unusual for George to sing through a complete score of one of his works, at the top of his voice. When his mother suggested that perhaps he ought not to be playing or singing his own works exclusively, he would say, "Then I'll not have a good time."

Despite this comment, George Gershwin was very modest about his own compositions and very enthusiastic about the work of other composers. He was always ready with a substantial check for some needy musician and he never overlooked a worthy cause. He was generous with his family and with his friends and he was never too busy to see people who wanted his advice or help.

George Gershwin was bored with vacations and was always happiest when working. He was especially fond of sports, though, and was seen at times at baseball games and fights. He lived comfortably, but simply, and often joked about his major extravagance — imported cigars.

In 1936, George Gershwin was invited to come to Hollywood to write music for the movies. It was there that he wrote his Second Rhapsody which joined "American in Paris" and Rhapsody in Blue as his best and most popular works. In Hollywood he also started to paint as a hobby and surprised himself and his friends with the results. A well-respected artist who saw George Gershwin's canvases, said that if he had spent as much time on painting as he had on music, he would have been one of America's top-notch painters.

On the eleventh of July, 1937, at the age of thirty-nine, George Gershwin died in Hollywood of a brain tumor. The world mourned the passing of this great American composer and wondered what compositions might have come from his pen had he lived longer than his very brief life. Only a genius could have accomplished so much in so short a time. He wrote music for the movies, for the stage, for the jazz band and the blues singer, and for the large symphony orchestra. The Russian composer Dmitri Kabelevsky best expresses Gershwin's contribution to the world of music when he says, "Gershwin contributed to the world's music not just his talent and part of himself but something far more important — a part of the American culture, American art."

Morton Gould

---

born in Richmond Hill, New York,
December 10, 1913

MORTON GOULD was the son of a real estate dealer and the oldest of four boys. At the time when most youngsters of four or five were playing cowboys and riding their bicycles, he preferred to sit at the piano and play tunes. When he was not happy with a tune he knew, he changed it to his liking. Once, after hearing Sousa's stirring march "The Stars and Stripes Forever" played by a band, he cried, "This is good music!" and surprised his family by playing it for them on the piano. His first composition, "Waltz for Piano," was published when he was only six years old.

The Institute of Musical Art in New York accepted Gould as a scholarship student when he was eight, and at thirteen he began to study piano with Miss Abby Whiteside. She found her pupil eager and hard-working and he covered as much material in one month as most pupils can cover in a year. His lessons were always well-prepared, and his interest never seemed to lag.

By the time he was fifteen years old, Morton Gould had completed a two-year course in composition and theory with Dr. Vincent Jones at New York University. He played in public when in his early teens and attracted

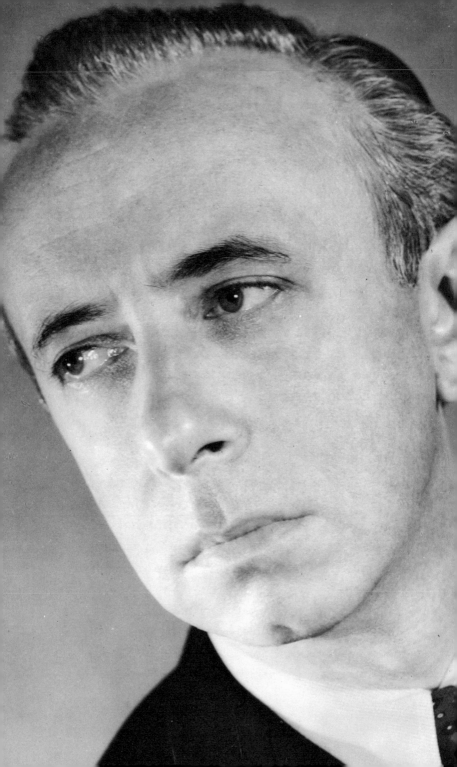

a great deal of attention because of his unusual technique as a pianist.

Because there was little money in the Gould family and there were three younger brothers who were too young to work, it was necessary for Morton Gould to earn his living before he was eighteen years old. To do so he played the piano in bands, theaters, movie houses, clubs, or any other place where a pianist was needed.

At eighteen he was engaged as staff pianist for Radio City Music Hall. This was a position of great responsibility, especially for someone so young, and he worked very hard at it. He did so well that three years later he was invited to conduct an orchestra over the Mutual Network, Station WOR. This was a wonderful opportunity for the young man. He could arrange his own program and build the orchestra as he wished to. As there was no television then, people listened to the radio as they now watch television.

Mr. Gould soon became famous for the programs he gave the public and for building a fine orchestra. He arranged music especially for the group and he rehearsed the musicians so well that his broadcasts rapidly became popular across the nation.

Mr. Gould is one of the most talented and versatile American musicians. He is well known as an outstanding composer of both serious and popular music, as an excellent pianist and as a conductor of unusual skill. In his symphonic works or concertos for solo instruments, he often adopts, with great skill and wit, tunes, rhythms, and harmonies from American folklore and jazz. He is popular with people who like good symphonic music and with high-school and college students who like good jazz. Also, he manages to combine the classical with jazz to create music that is typically American in style and taste.

In his "Cowboy Rhapsody" and "Foster Gallery" he uses American folk songs and the songs of Stephen Foster. His popular work "American Salute," written in 1942, was based on the old, catchy, marching melody of Civil War days, "When Johnny Comes Marching Home." His great interest in American history resulted in his writing "A Lincoln Legend," which was introduced by the great conductor Arturo Toscanini and the NBC Symphony Orchestra.

Another work, "Spirituals" for Orchestra is based on some of the most beautiful Negro spirituals. The composition was first introduced at the American Music Festival in 1941, with Mr. Gould conducting. In this work, the strings are the voices of a church choir, while the other instruments of the orchestra are the accompanying voices of the worshippers.

To prove that he does not always have to borrow either style or thematic material from folk songs and other sources, Mr. Gould has written large important works in which his own creative powers are in the forefront. He has written three symphonies, four "American Symphonettes," a "Latin American Symphonette," a *Concerto for Viola*, a *Piano Concerto* and a *Concerto for Orchestra* which he composed for the fortieth anniversary of the Cleveland

Orchestra. The composer has also written music for films. His music is charming, alive, tuneful, and very popular with audiences of all ages.

Despite his enormous success as composer and performer, Mr. Gould and his family live rather simply in Forest Hills, New York. He spends many hours a day working, and says, "I work on a million things at once, and I am always rushing to meet deadlines." When asked why he does not take a vacation, his reply is always the same, "I would not know what to do with it, never having had one."

Morton Gould has always been interested in railroads and has a fine picture collection of them. He once confessed to one of his friends that "next to being a musician, I might have liked to become a railroad engineer." He is an avid reader and is especially fond of books dealing with history and biography. Mr. Gould enjoys the movies and sees more films than the average person. He also listens frequently to the music of other composers and is a great admirer of the late George Gershwin.

Charles Griffes

born in Elmira, New York, September 17, 1884,
died in New York City, April 8, 1920

CHARLES TOMLINSON GRIFFES's life was not long enough
for him to prove himself the composer he might have been
if he had lived beyond his thirty-six years. He was born
in Elmira, New York, where he spent a happy childhood
with his parents and brother and sisters. From the time he
was a very small boy he liked bright colors and showed a
remarkable artistic talent. He was always a highly imaginative child and could imitate bird calls and sounds that
amazed his family. His sister Katherine was studying
piano with the hope of becoming a piano teacher, and it
was she who gave her younger brother his first piano lessons.
His progress was so rapid that she often had to ask her own
piano teacher what she should assign him for lessons, or
how to finger certain pieces he was learning.

When he was almost fifteen years old he had surpassed
his sister on the piano, and it was decided that young
Charles was to have his own lessons from Katherine's
teacher. Thus, he came into contact with Mary Selena
Broughton who not only gave him a very good background
in piano, but also had a great deal of influence on her
young pupil. Before he had finished high school, Charles
Griffes decided to become a concert pianist.

Miss Broughton soon learned that Charles had exceptional ability, and made it possible for him to study piano in Berlin, Germany. In addition to his piano study there, he also had theory lessons with Humperdinck, the composer of *Hansel and Gretel*. He, too, was quick to recognize the unusual ability of his pupil and urged him to become a composer.

The four years that Charles Griffes spent in Germany were productive and inspiring. Much influenced by his teachers, and steeped in the Romantic tradition, he wrote his first works in the style of the Romantic composers. Many of the lovely songs which he composed at that time are very much in the manner of Brahms and Schubert.

The music of the French impressionists Maurice Ravel and Claude Debussy opened new vistas to the young composer. The dream-like colorful quality of their music touched him deeply. The Russian school of composition, with which he came in contact for the first time, also intrigued him and critics found clear evidence of both the French and the Russian influences in some of his works. While this may be true, Charles Griffes was not one who followed styles rigidly, and he was certainly not one to copy. Basically the poetic and musical ideas were always his own.

In 1907, at the age of twenty-three, Mr. Griffes returned from Germany with a large number of works in his folio. He obtained a job as music teacher at the Hackley School for Boys in Tarrytown, New York. He taught, and played piano for assemblies, and organ for Sunday Church services.

His small apartment on the school grounds was a popular meeting place for students and faculty, who came to hear him play on Sunday evenings.

Griffes remained at the school until his death, thirteen years later, and the largest portion of his works was written in his small, crowded school studio. He wrote there all of the piano works which were done between the years 1910 and 1918.

During his short life time, Charles Griffes produced a large number of works which include songs, piano music, chamber music, and orchestral music full of poetry and rare imagination. Many of his compositions have been published and are recorded and performed by major symphony orchestras.

"The White Peacock" is part of "Roman Sketches," a group of descriptive pieces for piano. This work was inspired by poems written by a little-known Scotch poet. Of this work someone said, "Rarely has a composer translated from word to tone with such perfection." Mr. Griffes arranged the piano piece for orchestra and he follows the poems beautifully, giving voice to the different instruments which recite it. The "white" tones are given to the oboe, the "silver" tones to the flute, and the harp and celesta are used to express the shimmering of "warmth and light."

One of his most significant works, "The Pleasure-Dome of Kubla Khan," was originally intended as a piano composition when the composer began it in 1912. Not long afterwards, he changed his mind and wrote it for orchestra. In 1919, a year before his death, the Boston Symphony

Orchestra informed him that the work was scheduled to be played at one of their concerts. Mr. Griffes was pleased but concerned. The parts for the orchestra were not yet copied. Because it would cost more than he could afford to have them copied, he set to work and often worked far into the night. He kept at the task, in spite of his busy teaching schedule, until all the parts were copied.

Along with the music, Mr. Griffes sent the following note to the Boston Symphony Orchestra. "I have taken as a basis for my work those lines of Coleridge's poem describing 'the stately pleasure dome.' It might be well to quote in the program book some of these lines, at least the last six."

> The shadow of the dome of pleasure
> Floated midway on the waves;
> Where was heard the mingled measure
> From the fountain and the caves.
> It was a miracle of rare device,
> A sunny pleasure-dome with caves of ice.

In this work, Charles Griffes shows his enthusiasm for, and the influence of oriental music. It is an altogether lovely, colorful, and beautifully presented oriental fantasy.

On the 28th of November in 1919, Charles Griffes, tired but happy, heard "The Pleasure-Dome of Kubla Khan" performed by the Boston Symphony Orchestra under the direction of Pierre Monteux. The work was very well received and the composer was called to the stage for several bows. The following week it was performed at Carnegie Hall in New York by the same orchestra and the critics were equally enthusiastic.

Other orchestras and soloists were performing his music and Charles Griffes had every reason to be pleased and happy, but he had been ill since his return from Boston. Weeks in bed in Tarrytown followed. Then there was a long stay at Loomis Sanatorium from which he was moved to a hospital in New York City. On April 8th, 1920, Charles Griffes died of a chest infection. He was buried two days later in Bloomfield, New Jersey.

An editorial in the *New York Times* shortly after his death had this to say: "Mr. Griffes underwent for many years the drudgery of teaching in a boy's school which necessarily left him little leisure for composition. . . . We speak with pity and scorn of a public that could let a Mozart or a Schubert die and think that these bad old days are gone, but from time to time something uncomfortably like them and of the same sort is revealed in the present."

Ferde Grofé

born in New York City, March 12, 1892

WHEN WE REALIZE that Ferde Grofé's grandfather was a cello soloist with the Metropolitan Opera Company, his father a singer in light opera, his mother a gifted cellist and his uncle concert-master of the Los Angeles Symphony, it is not surprising that he, too, should have become a musician. Before he was five years old, he was placed on a piano stool and encouraged to play and, before he was able to write his name, his mother was teaching him to write music. When he was five years old, formal lessons on the violin and piano were started.

The boy was surrounded by musicians and spent most of his time on music, yet, when he expressed his decision to become a professional musician, his mother pleaded with him to consider business instead. Her son, however, could not be convinced.

After his father died, Ferde's mother remarried, and his stepfather was even less sympathetic to music as a career for him. At the age of fourteen, tired of all the arguments about his spending so much time on music, Ferde took matters into his own hands and ran away from home. In order to support himself, he took jobs as an elevator boy, milkman, truck driver, and as a worker in a book bindery. These jobs took all his time and energy

and left him little for practice, and certainly no money with which to pay for music lessons.

Ferde Grofé finally joined a cornet player with whom he traveled from town to town playing cornet and piano solos. The association was an unhappy one, however, for the cornet player left him stranded in a small town in northern California with unpaid bills for Ferde to pay.

Determined that he could be happy only in music, Ferde Grofé took the only music job that he could find, playing the piano in noisy, crowded cabarets or night-clubs. This action finally convinced his family of his earnestness and of his need for music, and they offered him assistance. The boy returned home and studied violin and composition. Ferde became a member of the violin section of the Los Angeles orchestra where he remained for ten years. The symphony season was not a long one — the orchestra members worked only twenty-five or twenty-eight weeks out of the year — and the pay checks were not very large. Ferde Grofé found he had to do other things to make ends meet, so he became a banjo player with one of the first ragtime bands to play on the West Coast.

Next he organized his own band and attracted attention with the special musical arrangements he made of the popular pieces of the day. The arrangements were unusual, and, when the famous band leader Paul Whiteman heard them, he immediately engaged Grofé as his pianist and arranger. For the next ten years every note played by this very popular jazz band was arranged by Grofé.

Ferde Grofé knew instruments and how to use them.

He knew how to combine instrumental sounds to produce effects which amazed audiences. He took some of the raucous, unbearable noise out of jazz and raised the jazz band to the concert level. The Whiteman-Grofé combination was a great success on the coast and it soon was decided to take the band to New York with the idea of giving jazz concerts. It was at the first of these concerts, in Aeolian Hall, that George Gershwin's *Rhapsody in Blue* was presented. It was arranged by Grofé in only ten days.

In 1924 Ferde Grofé left Paul Whiteman's band to do free-lance arranging and to devote himself to composition. His search for musical realism resulted in some unusual and unique effects. In his work "Tabloid," a picture of newspaper life, he uses an actual typewriter as one of the instruments in the orchestra. In his *Symphony in Steel* sirens and drills are heard as part of the musical story and in "Free Air" a bicycle pump is used. As would be fitting for *Hollywood Suite*, the banging of the carpenters' hammers fixing scenery is heard along with the shouting of the director. These are most unusual methods of presenting realism in music, for Mr. Grofé has never hesitated to use every possible means at his disposal in order to produce a desired effect.

Perhaps Grofé's most important and best known work is his *Grand Canyon Suite*, which he composed in 1931. This work has been played by most of the orchestras in this country and is considered a most important American composition. Though the jazz technique which Mr. Grofé employs in most of his works is also found here, it differs greatly from his other compositions. It is perhaps his most original score. The music is descriptive, without resorting to the realism of non-musical, mechanical instruments. It is refined music, and, as though taking a tour of the Grand Canyon or seeing a painting, the listener can almost visualize the brilliant colors of this masterpiece of nature. This suite is divided into five parts entitled "Sunrise," "The Painted Desert," "On the Trail," "Sunset," and "Cloudburst." As one listens to the entire suite, an impression is created of an early morning sunrise followed by the hours to eventide when the shadows cover the pink and purple of the canyon, and the sun fades in a mantle of darkness. "On the Trail" is perhaps the most popular of the five movements as it depicts a cowboy descending one of the hazardous paths in the canyon, singing a cowboy song against the rhythmic jogging of the burro. "Cloudburst" is one of the most descriptive storm scenes ever created in music.

Mr. Grofé has of recent years become known as a conductor as well as a composer and arranger. In 1937 he conducted a concert devoted to his music at Carnegie Hall, and he has since appeared with many leading orchestras in the dual role of composer-conductor. He has written music for films and ballet, chamber music, and a choral work entitled "Uncle Sam Stands Up." It is of interest to note that two of Grofé's major works were commissioned by industry. *Symphony in Steel* was commissioned by the American Rolling Mills Company and *Wheels* by the Ford Motor Company.

It has been said that a good way to learn about American

regional history is to listen to the music of Grofé. He has written suites about the Hudson and the Mississippi Rivers, about Death Valley, the Grand Canyon, and San Francisco. This last work written for, and first performed by the San Francisco Symphony Orchestra, traces the history of the city from gold-rush days to the present. It is a wonderfully descriptive work in which the clanging of the cable car bells, Chinese gongs, and fog horns are heard just as they are when one visits this cosmopolitan city.

Mr. Grofé lives in Santa Monica, California. He is short, of heavy build, and spends much time out-of-doors. He is constantly writing things in his notebook — ideas, rhythms, or tunes for a new composition. "When an idea comes," he says, "I put salt on its tail before it can fly away."

Howard Hanson

born in Wahoo, Nebraska, October 20, 1896

No American musician has ever been more active in behalf of American music than Dr. Howard Hanson. Composer, conductor, teacher, administrator, lecturer, and friend of young musicians, he was born of Swedish parents and was reared in a community largely settled by Swedish pioneers. At the age of seven he began to study music and to compose and, by the time he was in high school, knew what he wanted to become.

In high school his very favorite composers were Handel and Grieg and he devoted a lot of time to studying their works. At Luther College he majored in music and upon graduation, continued his studies of piano and composition at the Institute of Musical Art in New York City. Then he went on to attend Northwestern University where his work in the academic subjects was equally as good as his work in music.

At nineteen he received his degree and the following year he accepted a position as professor of theory and composition at the College of the Pacific in San Jose, California. Three years later, before his twenty-third birthday, he was appointed Dean of the Conservatory of Fine Arts of that college.

In 1921 Howard Hanson won the "Prix de Rome" in

composition. It made it possible for him to spend three years at the American Academy in Rome where some of his important musical works were written. Upon his return to the United States in 1924, he was appointed Director of the Eastman School of Music of the University of Rochester, in Rochester, New York.

During his directorship over the last thirty-nine years, Dr. Hanson helped the Eastman School of Music develop into one of our very best schools of music. He has taught composition to countless young composers. His interest in the creative gifts of young musicians is genuine and, through the "Annual Festival of New Music" which he founded, he has introduced many young gifted composers to this country.

Dr. Hanson is a rare person, capable of doing many things well. Besides his many musical activities, he has served often as judge at many music competitions, has been advisor to the United States government on cultural matters, has written for many professional magazines, and has lectured to audiences all over the country. His book, *Harmonic Materials of Modern Music*, is a fine contribution to this field of musical literature.

Dr. Hanson has also distinguished himself as a guest conductor of many of our major symphony orchestras, conducting his own works and the works of other American composers. He has conducted in Finland, and in 1933 he was invited by the pre-Hitler German government to conduct some of that country's leading orchestras in the works of American composers.

As a composer, Dr. Hanson has written music for the large symphony orchestra, chamber music in various combinations of instruments, choral works, and stage works. The first of his five symphonies, the *Nordic*, was introduced in Rome, and brought him to national prominence. This symphony sings of the grandeur of the north. His second symphony, the *Romantic*, was commissioned by the Boston Symphony Orchestra in 1930 for its fiftieth anniversary season. This work is a definite rebellion against the style of composing that then prevailed. The "romantic" period had come to an end perhaps thirty years earlier, and the composer felt that "the emotional element of music had been shunted aside." The *Romantic Symphony* "represents my escape from the rather bitter type of modern musical realism," he says.

Hanson's *Third Symphony* was a tribute to the early Swedish pioneers who settled in Delaware in 1638, and the *Fourth Symphony* was written in memory of his father. Many of the composer's works have been commissioned, including "Mosaics" which was written for the fortieth anniversary of the Cleveland Orchestra. His opera "Merry Mount," was performed at the Metropolitan Opera House in 1934.

In speaking of his own music, Howard Hanson says, "I am a natural composer. I write music because I have to write it. Though I have a profound interest in theoretical problems, my own music comes 'from the heart' and is a direct expression of my own emotional reactions."

Dr. Hanson is tall, a little stoop-shouldered and, despite the beard which he grew as a young man to make him look older, he looks extremely youthful. With Mrs. Hanson he lives in Rochester, where much of their time is spent at the Eastman School of Music. Dr. Hanson has a fine sense of humor; he is casual, informal, and friendly. Most of all, he is always ready with a word of encouragement or advice to the many music students at the Eastman School, or to young musicians anywhere.

Roy Harris

---

born in Lincoln County, Oklahoma,
February 12, 1898

It is hard to believe that Roy Harris, named Leroy Ellsworth Harris at birth, could have lived in a log cabin built by his parents! It is, however, true. His parents were pioneers, and their son, born on Lincoln's birthday, lived the life of a pioneer for the first five years of his life.

Then, because the Oklahoma climate did not agree with the elder Harrises, they packed their belongings and moved to California. There they settled on a farm in the San Gabriel Valley. Farming was hard work for all the family and Roy did his share. At ten, he had his own garden and was earning his keep by selling vegetables and eggs to people in the community. He always found time for reading and studying, however, and he frequently surprised his parents and friends with his wide interests and knowledge.

When Roy was fourteen years old, two very exciting things happened to him — he entered high school, and the Harris family bought an upright piano. At this time, a piano was not a common thing in the community and hardly anyone but his mother knew how to play it. Roy was delighted with it and, though he took no lessons, he spent much time beating out different tunes and rhythms he knew. Almost every day he found it easier to find the

right keys. He was having a wonderful time at the piano, until he discovered that his friends were making fun of him. To prove that he was no sissy, he changed his name to Roy and began playing football. His reward for the latter effort was to break his nose, his left arm and the fourth finger of his right hand. After that, either no one ever again made fun of him, or he did not care, for not only did he spend time at the piano but he also started to take clarinet lessons.

It was not until he was twenty years old that Roy Harris began to study music seriously at the University of California. There he studied harmony and was convinced for the first time that, above everything else, he wanted to write music. He had to do outside work while attending classes and found a job as a truck driver delivering butter and eggs for a dairy company. Much of his work had to be done before classes started and Mr. Harris got used to getting up at four or five in the morning. To this day, he still finds that his best hours for work are those between five and nine A.M.

After only two years of composition study with Modeste Altschuler he wrote the "Andante" for orchestra. It was performed by the New York Philharmonic under van Hoogstraten at the Stadium Concerts. Harris was so anxious to hear the work played that he hitchhiked to New York. He arrived with five dollars in his pocket. Things did not go well thereafter. He worked for a short time in a settlement house and then decided to return to California. There he became music critic for the Los

Angeles *Illustrated Daily* and also taught harmony at the Hollywood Conservatory of Music.

In 1926 Mr. Harris went to Paris to study with Nadia Boulanger, the fine teacher of many other American composers. For three years he worked with her and during this period wrote his first major work, the *Concerto for Piano, String Quartet and Clarinet.*

An accident which fractured the young composer's spine made it necessary for him to return to America for surgery and a long stay in the hospital. There he could not compose at the piano, so he started to work without it and, to his great amazement, found that he could compose with greater speed than before. The first work he produced away from the piano was a string quartet. He was delighted with it and, when he was well again, Mr. Harris could often be found with his music pad, sitting on a log, rock, or the green grass, putting his thoughts on paper. He often speaks of this accident as a blessing which advanced his composing time by ten years!

Mr. Harris, listed as one of America's top-notch composers, has an impressive list of compositions to his name. He has written eight symphonies, string quartets and other chamber music, cantatas, concertos for piano and for violin, choral and band music for schools and universities, as well as many other works. He is the first American composer to have had a work commissioned for recording before it was publicly played. This was his "The American Overture" based on the well-known Civil War tune, "When Johnny Comes Marching Home," which he first

heard his father whistle. His Third Symphony was introduced by the Boston Symphony Orchestra under the baton
of Koussevitzky. His Fourth Symphony was written for
Tommy Dorsey's jazz orchestra. *The San Francisco Symphony*, his eighth symphony, was commissioned by the
San Francisco Symphony Orchestra in celebration of the
orchestra's fiftieth season. The composer started the work
while flying in a plane across the country at an altitude
of 33,000 feet! It takes twenty-two minutes to play this
symphony that took the composer one month to compose.

Roy Harris has had great influence on American music,
not only through his compositions, but because he has
trained many young musicians. He has taught composition at a number of colleges, including Westminster Choir
School, Princeton and Cornell Universities, Colorado
College, and Indiana University. His music is typically
American — it speaks of the prairies of Kansas and
Nebraska, and is at times sprinkled with a nostalgic folk
tune. It is easy to listen to, has melody and most of it is
fresh and not complicated.

Mr. Harris has the unusual ability to work on several
different compositions at the same time. Once he
starts a composition, he is restless until it is finished. He
often gets up at three in the morning and works for an
eighteen-hour stretch. He permits nothing to interfere
with his composing. Several years ago, an automobile
accident smashed his right knee into twenty pieces. Though
at times he was pretty uncomfortable, he continued to
compose in the hospital, and produced there one of his

longest and best works, the *Folk Fantasy for Festival*, which takes fifty-five minutes to play.

Roy Harris looks like a westerner. He slouches, wears his clothes in a casual manner, and there is no pretense about him. His great joy is reading and, since his music is so often based on American facts and personalities, he does a great deal of it. Before writing his *Abraham Lincoln Symphony*, he read many Lincoln biographies, and his music shows the effects of his thorough research.

Although Mr. Harris is guest lecturer at the University of California, he is a resident of Puerto Rico, where he teaches at the Inter-American University. He and his wife Johana, a brilliant pianist, are always surrounded by their children, students, and the sound of music. The Harrises have great understanding of young people and their needs. It was not at all uncommon for either one of them to teach and feed needy students in exchange for baby-sitting or car-washing. Mrs. Harris is devoted to her husband's music and she is usually the first to play it publicly. They live simply, work hard, and have little time for hobbies. Mr. Harris loves a game of chess, or tennis, which he no longer plays.

Perhaps the citation which Mr. Harris received from the governor of Colorado on his fiftieth birthday sums up anything else we might want to say about him.

"As a composer, you have given our schools, churches, and concert halls American music which characterizes our people and our time; as a teacher, you have spoken to students throughout America of the worth and dignity of

American culture, and you have, by your own example, given encouragement to them to create and play the vital new music of this free and democratic land."

Alan Hovhaness

born in Somerville, Massachusetts, March 8, 1911

ALAN HOVHANESS, a most unusual and prolific composer, is the son of Armenian and Scottish parents. His father, Haroutin Hovhaness Chakmakjian, was a professor of chemistry. His mother, Madeline Scott Chakmakjian, did not want her son "tied down" to a strange long foreign name and, before he realized what his name really was, she had it officially changed to Alan Hovhaness. When he was five years old, the family moved to Arlington, a suburb of Boston, where he grew up.

Music held a great fascination for Alan Hovhaness, and, as soon as he had learned to read it, he began to compose. When he studied piano in Boston, he was encouraged by his teachers to become a solo pianist, but composing interested him more than performing. After a brief period of study in composition at the New England Conservatory of Music he was determined to devote himself to composition. In 1942 he received a scholarship to study with the well-known composer Martinu at Tanglewood, Massachusetts.

For several years Mr. Hovhaness taught music in Boston, and from 1948 to 1951 he was a member of the faculty of the Boston Conservatory of Music. Because he found that a heavy teaching schedule did not allow much

time for composing, Mr. Hovhaness in 1951 decided to move to New York City and devote all his time to creating music.

This proved to be a very wise decision, for, in a period of ten years, he has received many prizes, awards, and commissions, and has written a large number of works that have been performed by major orchestras in America and Europe. In 1951 he received an award for outstanding compositions from the National Institute of Arts and Letters. Two Guggenheim Fellowships followed, in 1953 and 1955, which made it possible for him to travel to Greece. The Fromm Foundation commissioned him to compose a work for chorus and orchestra. Another commissioned work, "Ardent Song," was used by the famous dancer Martha Graham and her company of dancers, and was performed both here and in Europe.

This composer has also had a commission from the Houston Symphony Orchestra, for which he wrote one of his largest works, *Ad Lyram*, for solo voice, double chorus, and orchestra. His well-known and popular *Easter Cantata* was written for the Columbia Broadcasting Company. In 1954 he wrote the music to Clifford Odets' *The Flowering Peach*, which was performed on Broadway. He also was commissioned by NBC to compose a score for the documentary film, "Assignment in India," which was shown on television and in theaters in the Far East.

Even though Mr. Hovhaness has destroyed most of the music that he wrote before 1940, because he was dissatisfied with it, the composer estimates that he has written close to 1200 works, including sixteen symphonies. Many of these compositions are in constant demand for performance all over the world. According to a survey of the programs of seventy-four symphony orchestras for the 1959–60 season, Mr. Hovhaness's "Mysterious Mountain" was performed more often than any one work by any other American composer.

Mr. Hovhaness is one of the most interesting and often most baffling of musicians. Although his early works showed some influence of Sibelius, he has since found his very own means of expressing himself in his music. There is no doubt that he is much influenced by his own Armenian background, and especially by experiences he had as a young man. When he was church organist at an Armenian church in Boston, he heard the old chants and songs founded on the traditions of his father's ancestors. And in his own music he has captured the simplicity, flavor, and fascinating rhythms of Armenian church and folk music.

The composer has also found much inspiration and material in his travels, especially in India and Japan. Perhaps this may account for some of his works being described as "oriental-sounding."

Despite the many different influences, the music of Alan Hovhaness is original, inspiring, uncomplicated, and individual. He shows that he has mastered the techniques of writing music, and he is not afraid to use old devices and sounds that are strange and different. Also, he is a master creator of mood through the use of instruments, especially those of the percussion family, the harp, and the celesta. Like a painter, he designs and creates musical patterns for the listening ear.

Mr. Hovhaness is a tall, moustached, dark-haired, dark-eyed gentleman with sharp facial features. He dresses casually, is an attentive listener, and a slow careful speaker. He has few hobbies, and spends most of his time composing. His commissions are many, and he writes music for groups and for individuals at rather short notice. He is often so busy finishing a composition he has promised, that he does not have time to attend the concerts to hear his works performed. He is extremely fond of cats and at least one of them, "Baba," was at his side, snuggled close to him, as he wrote some of his best compositions.

Perhaps the best description of Alan Hovhaness as a composer is given by Rudolph Elie of the Boston *Herald*, who reviewed the premiere of his *Easter Cantata* on May 11, 1955. "The Boston premiere of Alan Hovhaness' 'Easter Cantata' last night revealed again the special qualities that more and more indicate the emergence of this composer's stature as one of the few truly born composers in the land. There are many gifted ones . . . yet it is seldom indeed that their music strikes the note of inspiration, of coming directly from a wellspring so deep and so urgent as to be irrepressible. He began writing music at Mozart's age and has never done anything else. The resulting body of his work today is perfectly enormous, probably exceeding 200 opus by far, and of uniformly high character."

Charles Ives

born in Danbury, Connecticut, October 20, 1874,
died in New York City, May 19, 1954

CHARLES IVES was the son of a bandmaster in General Grant's army. His father was a thorough musician and taught him theory, harmony, and counterpoint. It was somewhat of a game for father and son to explore the vast field of music — to experiment with notes on the piano, to form new and different chords. When he was thirteen years old, Charles Ives wrote his first composition, "A Holiday Quickstep," which was performed by the town band. The next year he was hired as "the youngest organist in the state" to play in the First Baptist Church of Danbury.

After the death of his father, Charles continued his studies with Dudley Buck and Horatio Parker at Yale University. He was a very good student and showed an unusual independence in his compositions, often shocking his teachers by using "strange" harmonies and rhythms. In 1898, the year that he was graduated from Yale, all his friends expected that he would continue working in the field of music but, to their great surprise, he took a job as a clerk in an insurance agency. In 1909 he formed his own insurance company and became a most successful businessman.

To the world it looked as if Charles Ives had deserted music forever and was devoting all of his energies to his business. The impression, however, was false because during all the years he spent as a businessman, Ives continued to experiment in music. He wrote the bulk of his major compositions during this period.

Charles Ives was an individualist who did not follow the existing rules for composing. In his music he tried to express his own experiences and feelings as an American. He was not afraid of harsh, clashing chords and he used American folk tunes, marches, dances, and hymns in such a way that they became original parts of his own compositions. In speaking of Ives' *Symphony No. 2*, a reviewer says, "Throughout its five movements, quotations from such tunes as 'Columbia, the Gem of the Ocean,' Foster's 'Camptown Races' and 'Bringing in the Sheaves,' keep cropping up . . . and yet, it is distinctly original in flavor."

Mr. Ives knew how to use the instruments of the orchestra and made use of their every possibility in the production of sound. He was able to combine musical themes — often using one against the other. Sometimes he had one group of instruments play in different rhythm — and even in a different key — all within the same composition.

For almost forty years Charles Ives was a businessman and a composer. He composed during his lunch hour, on weekends, and en route to and from work. His output of musical works is tremendous but, unfortunately, because he had little hope of having his works performed, he often wrote his scores in pencil, then stuffed them into bureau drawers, or discarded them. The few friends who knew about his compositions thought it a strange hobby for a successful businessman.

In 1930 Ives the insurance man retired because of ill health, and the world began to take notice of Ives the composer. His music came as a shock to many musicians. It was so modern, so daring. It was more advanced than the music of the well-known modernists Stravinsky, Bartók and Schoenberg whose music Ives had never heard. Suddenly Ives became "the first American composer with modern ideas." His music appeared on many concert programs, and American audiences began to hear for the first time works written many years earlier.

In May of 1946, Ives was honored with a program devoted to his music presented at the Columbia Festival of Contemporary Music. His Third Symphony, written in 1911, which had never been heard before, was awarded the Pulitzer Prize. His famous *Concord Sonata*, written between 1911 and 1915, became a favorite of pianists. His charming piece for orchestra, "The Unanswered Question," written in 1908, was performed by the New York Philharmonic Orchestra on its tour of the Soviet Union in August 1959. Leonard Bernstein took several minutes to talk to the Russian audiences about this short composition which he felt was an important one and representative of American music. The little composition, which lasts only about five minutes, is considered a masterpiece of workmanship and is often referred to as a "mood piece."

Mr. Ives' works include five symphonies, sonatas for

violin and piano, chamber music works, and more than 120 fine songs. Programs all over the country now carry the name of Charles Ives. His compositions are performed and appreciated, but it is sad to think that musical recognition should have come when he was almost sixty years old and not well enough to really enjoy the honors paid him.

Perhaps Charles Ives was at least partially responsible for the neglect of his works and for the lack of recognition given him. He was an extremely shy and modest person who did not like to speak about himself or his work and was much afraid of publicity. He hated to be photographed and there are very few pictures of him taken during his long lifetime.

Charles Ives was an individual in every way. He did not follow any styles or customs of dress or appearance. His heavy beard always attracted attention wherever he was seen and his battered hat, thick shoes, and rumpled clothing made him look like anything but a successful businessman or musician. He rarely went out or had visitors, seldom read a newspaper, and refused to own either a record player or a radio.

Charles Ives died on May 19, 1954, in New York City, at the age of eighty. He had been writing music since he was a very young man and many of his major works date back to his early years when he was in his twenties and early thirties. It was nearly forty years before he heard any of it performed.

Ulysses Kay

---

born in Tucson, Arizona,, January 7, 1917

Ulysses Kay, who was born in Tucson, Arizona, was the son of a barber. His father, when he was not busy in his shop, was forever singing and beating out rhythms to amuse and entertain his children. His mother loved to sing and played the piano well. The boy's earliest recollections of home are connected with music: his mother singing as she worked, his older sister practicing Chopin and Rachmaninoff, his brother playing the fiddle. When Ulysses was ten, his brother stopped playing the violin in order to devote more time to the saxophone, and the violin was "passed on" to him. By then Ulysses had had some lessons on the piano but he also thoroughly enjoyed studying the violin. When his older sister bought him a saxophone two years later, he practiced on three different instruments, but still he had no positive idea that he wanted to be become a musician.

In high school Ulysses participated in many musical activities. He sang in the glee club, played in the marching band, and was a member of the school dance orchestra. His first year at a liberal arts college did not satisfy him. He missed music too much, so he changed to the music school and majored in public school music. His piano

teacher there was Julia Rebeil, and both she and John L. Lowell, with whom Ulysses studied theory, at once recognized his musical gifts.

In 1938, he was graduated from the University of Arizona with a scholarship to the Eastman School of Music in Rochester, New York. There he studied composition with Howard Hanson and Bernard Rogers. Later, a scholarship at Tanglewood, Massachusetts, resulted in his study of composition with the eminent composer Paul Hindemith, with whom he continued to study on a scholarship at Yale University.

The war interrupted Ulysses' studies. He enlisted in the United States Navy and was assigned to a band stationed in Rhode Island, where he served from 1942 to 1946. In the Navy he played saxophone and piano in the dance orchestra; he learned to play the flute and the piccolo, and made many interesting arrangements for the band.

Mr. Kay's first composition was a set of ten piano pieces for children, which he wrote when he was twenty-two years old. The following year he wrote his first important orchestral works, a "Sinfonietta," an "Oboe Concerto," and "Five Mosaics for Chamber Orchestra." These brought him to the forefront as one of America's most gifted young composers.

His list of compositions is a very impressive one, for it consists only of works which the composer feels are worthy of being placed before the public. He is highly critical of his own writing, and has not permitted a number of his works to be performed or published. He does not feel that they represent his best effort.

Mr. Kay's works are strongly rhythmical, dramatic, and full of strength and vitality. In recognition of his talents, he has received two Rosenwald fellowships and two fellowships at the American Academy in Rome, besides many cash prizes. In 1954, his native town, Tucson, invited him to conduct the Tucson Symphony Orchestra in his own symphonic score *New Horizons*. In 1958, he was one of the four American composers selected to visit the Soviet Union under the U.S. State Department Cultural, Educational, and Technical Exchange. There he received high praise for his *New Horizons*.

Mr. Kay has written a large number of works for orchestra, string orchestra, chorus, band, chamber orchestra, organ, and piano. He has also written several operas, of which the best known is *The Boor*, a one-act opera based on the play by the Russian author Anton Chekhov. In addition to composing, Mr. Kay is a full-time employee of Broadcast Music, Inc., in their New York City office.

Undoubtedly among the most gifted of American composers, Ulysses Kay refuses to be labeled. He is a Negro composer who works in a broad, inspiring framework and who has created a large number of very unusual and beautiful musical works.

Normand Lockwood

born in New York City, March 19, 1906

WHEN NORMAND LOCKWOOD was a young child, his family moved from New York City where he was born, to Ann Arbor, Michigan. There his father taught piano at the University of Michigan, while he attended the public schools, and studied piano with his father. After completing high school he went to the University of Michigan where he majored in music.

He began to compose while still at college and, as soon as he was graduated, went to Europe to continue his studies in composition. In Italy he worked with the well-known Italian composer Ottorino Respighi, and in France his teacher was Nadia Boulanger, the teacher of so many other well-known composers. In 1929, the composer received a fellowship which made it possible for him to return to Italy and to study at the American Academy in Rome, where he remained until 1932. When he returned to the United States, he was a thoroughly schooled and accomplished composer.

Since few composers can earn a living from composing alone, Mr. Lockwood accepted a teaching position in the Conservatory of Music of Oberlin College, where he taught for about ten years. He has also taught at Columbia and Yale Universities and at a number of other schools as well.

Mr. Lockwood is a composer of rare ability. His music is fluent, with a good melodic line, has exciting rhythmical effects, and is often dramatic in concept. While it is contemporary in character, it also has a quality that is lasting and ageless. His choral work "Prairie," for chorus and orchestra, set to the words of the poet Carl Sandburg, well fits the drama and suspense of the poem. In the composition Lockwood drew on some musical themes and ideas from traditional Western songs. It was commissioned in 1953 for the sixtieth Ann Arbor May Festival.

The composer says about his music in general, "I have been making an increased effort to write music which . . . the memory will retain . . . I try chiefly to write in such a way, and with a degree of clarity that what is played, sung, and heard, will stick."

Mr. Lockwood has the ability to use American songs and folk tunes, often insignificant and drab, and weave them into fine and dignified works. His choral arrangements of American folk music are poetic and dramatic and yet retain their original American color and flavor. He says, "Who can say when composition begins and arranging leaves off?"

Although it is often said that few composers can turn out a chorus or a song with the artistry of Normand Lockwood, these are not the only areas of music in which he has shown mastery as a composer. Lockwood is also well known for his fine chamber music and his works for orchestra. Perhaps his *Concerto for Organ and Brasses* is the best proof that he can write in other media too.

Normand Lockwood has been the recipient of many prizes and fellowships and has had a number of commissions for works. In 1934 he won the Swift Orchestra Prize and the G. Schirmer World's Fair Prize for an unaccompanied chorus suitable for high-school voices. In 1939 he was commissioned by the Elizabeth Sprague Coolidge Foundation to write a trio for flute, viola, and harp. His full-length opera *The Scarecrow*, dealing with witchcraft, was commissioned by the Alice Ditson Fund and was completed in 1945. The Society for the Publication of American Music gave him an award for his Third String Quartet, and he has also been the winner of Guggenheim Fellowships in 1943 and in 1944.

As a composer, Mr. Lockwood differs from many others because he believes in writing practical, playable music. He is well aware of the limitations of both instruments and players. He also knows that rehearsal time, too, is often limited and he therefore feels that composers should do everything possible to cut technical difficulties to a minimum. "A piece should sound at the first reading," he believes, and should not be so difficult that it requires many rehearsals before it is ready for performance.

The composer has practiced well what he preaches. He has written, and has had published, a number of choral works which are very much within the range of most amateur groups. Some of these are intended for church choirs, others, like his "Apple Orchards," to the text of a poem by Walt Whitman, are suitable for school choruses.

The purpose of his "Six Serenades for Strings," written in 1945, is to provide a group of short pieces without technical difficulties for school programs.

Mr. Lockwood has also written a number of highly successful scores for children which are recorded: "Hiawatha," "The Travels of Babar," "Mickey Goes to School," "Animal Super Market," and "Riddle-Me-This." He has the gift of appealing to children without "talking down" to them musically, and in all of these works, he has made good use of his sense of the dramatic, his humor, and his ability to portray, by means of music, scenes and characters which children can both see and feel.

Normand Lockwood, a tall gentleman with horn-rimmed glasses, is seldom without his pipe, or without a twinkle in his eyes. Despite the fact that he was born, and lived most of his life in America, one wonders if he might not be an Englishman, upon hearing him speak. He is very fond of reading and walking. His three daughters are grown and live in different parts of the country. Mr. Lockwood, who loves the mountains, has taught music in different colleges in the west. He generally gives his address as Laramie, Wyoming.

Edward MacDowell

born in New York City, December 18, 1861,
died there January 23, 1908

W HEN HE WAS A LITTLE BOY, Edward MacDowell showed
such ability in drawing and painting, that those who saw
his work could hardly have believed that he would be
anything but an artist. Yet MacDowell proved that, though
he could excel in both art and music, he loved music more.

Edward MacDowell was born in New York City, and
lived there in a neat little three-story brick house, shaded
by maple trees, with his Quaker father, his mother, and his
brother Walter who was three years older. His father had
great interest in the arts and should have liked to devote
himself to drawing and painting. Music and art, however,
were considered frivolous by the Quakers and so he decided
to become a businessman.

Edward had a very happy childhood. His mother, who
had been a teacher in the New York City schools, saw to
it that her boys had good books and games, and that they
were well and happy. There were rides into the country
in horse-drawn carriages, and walks through Central Park,
followed by picnics. Edward was considered a handsome
child as well as an artistic one. He filled the margins of
his books with drawings of birds and trees and flowers.
He wrote verses and he loved to sing. He was highly

imaginative, and his fairy-tale characters were very real to him.

It was a difficult matter to decide whether to give Edward — or "Eddie" as the family called him — art or music lessons. He was eager for both, but his Quaker father disapproved of either. Mrs. MacDowell, however, convinced her husband that there was no harm in music lessons for a small boy and, at the age of eight he began to study piano. His first teacher was a friend of the family, a Columbian musician, Juan Buitrago. Edward studied with Señor Buitrago for several years until he informed the family that he had taught Edward all he could and that their son was in need of a more gifted teacher.

Another South American, the famous Venezuelan pianist Teresa Carreno, took him on as her pupil and it did not take her long to discover his great musical gifts. She also found a sure way of getting him to work hard for her — she told him that whenever he had a poor lesson she would kiss him!

When Edward was fifteen years old, the family decided that he was to go to Europe for more serious music study. In the spring of 1876, he and his mother left for Paris, where he became a student at the Paris Conservatory. After two years there he went to Frankfort and still he had no idea of becoming a composer. He hoped to become a piano soloist and was therefore very pleased with his teacher Carl Heymann, who told his pupils that he "dared to play the classics as if they were written by men with blood in their veins." He also studied composition with

Joachim Raff, who played an important part in guiding MacDowell's career. He recognized real talent in the "scribblings" of his young student and tried to convince him that there were many people who could play the piano but not many who could compose. Raff was determined to turn Edward's attention toward composing.

His First Piano Concerto was written shortly after he began to study with Raff, who was so delighted with it that he showed it to Franz Liszt. Liszt received the young composer, praised his concerto and invited him to play at the meeting of the Allgemeiner Deutscher Musikverein. This encouragement and praise gave MacDowell new courage and he began thinking of himself as a composer as well as a pianist.

After several years as a student, MacDowell began to teach piano and built up a large class of students. One of his pupils, an American girl named Marian Nevins interested him particularly and, in the summer of 1884, after an absence of eight years, he followed her back to the United States where they were married. In a short time, though, they were back in Germany where Edward again took up his work of teaching and composing. These four years which he and his wife spent near Wiesbaden were probably the happiest and most productive of his life. Piano pieces, songs, and compositions for orchestra came from his pen and delighted American and European performers and audiences.

In 1888 the MacDowells said goodbye to Germany and sailed for America. They had selected Boston as the place where they would live, and received a cordial reception there. Everyone was eager to hear the young composer, but MacDowell was reluctant to give a concert. He felt that his piano playing had suffered from the time he had spent on composing. Finally, though, he played in public some of his own compositions and those of other composers, and was an immediate success. Bostonians called him the poet-musician!

The years in Boston were happy ones for the Mac-Dowells. Settled in a comfortable small house, Edward liked to stay at home, read, practice, or compose. He refrained from going places where there were crowds and the summer of 1890 found him in need of a summer place where he could work without interruption. Their first visit to Peterboro, New Hampshire, made a most favorable impression on the MacDowells and for three happy, productive summers they rented a house there. It was their good fortune, in 1896, to buy a farm including almost seventy acres of land. It is this farm that is known as the MacDowell Colony, a haven for musicians, poets, authors, and artists who seek peace and quiet to work undisturbed.

MacDowell's fame as a composer and teacher spread rapidly and, when a director was needed for the newly formed music department of Columbia University, the job was offered to him as "the greatest musical genius America has produced." Edward MacDowell had high standards for the department.

There was not enough staff and he took it upon himself to teach many more courses than it was possible for one person to handle. He was an inspiring, tireless teacher but his hours of teaching, lecturing, and administrating made great demands on his energy. After eight years at the university, his friends could hardly recognize him. It was evident that what he was giving to the university was at a great sacrifice to his failing health. Finally, completely exhausted and discouraged, MacDowell resigned from Columbia. For a time he continued teaching and composing, but he grew weaker and his last days were spent in deep depression and poor health. On January 23, 1908, Edward MacDowell died and was buried on a hilltop in his beloved farm in Peterboro.

Edward MacDowell has written many compositions, about a third of them songs. His shorter pieces or sketches are unforgettable nature moods in which the composer speaks more eloquently than do many composers in compositions of greater length. He is spoken of as a "tone poet" whose melodies are fresh and appealing.

It is very hard to characterize MacDowell's style. One feels and senses his music and, when once heard, one seldom can forget "To a Water Lily," "To a Wild Rose," or "Starlight." His music almost always expresses a poetic idea, and he at times put a line of verse on the title page of his published works. Some of his other "miniature" compositions are "To the Sea," "From a Wandering Iceberg," and "In Mid Ocean."

His larger works are two piano concertos and four sonatas for piano which are still great favorites with pianists. The *Indian Suite* is MacDowell's second suite for full orchestra and is considered the most mature of his works. It was first performed by the Boston Symphony Orchestra, to which it is dedicated. MacDowell says of it that he had derived most of its themes from the tribal melodies of the North American Indians. This suite is in five movements: "Legend," "Love Song," "In War-time," "Dirge," and "Village Festival."

Edward MacDowell's music reflects his being, his personality. It is sincere, simple, often shy and sad, and at times bubbling over with humor. It describes the composer as he lived and died.

Peter Mennin

born in Erie, Pennsylvania, May 17, 1923

AT AN AGE when most people are hard at work getting "settled" in jobs or still striving to get a foothold on the ladder of success, Peter Mennin had reached the top. Before his fortieth birthday, he was regarded as one of America's outstanding composers, with a long list of fine works to his credit. When he was only thirty-five, he became director of the Peabody Conservatory of Music in Baltimore, Maryland. His fine leadership as administrator placed him in line four years later for an appointment as President of the Juilliard School of Music, a position previously held by the composer William Schuman.

Mr. Mennin's musical education started when he was seven years old and not long after that he began to write music, especially for piano and voice. At the age of seventeen, the Conservatory of Music of Oberlin College in Oberlin, Ohio, accepted him as a student. Here he studied composition with Normand Lockwood.

During his brief stay at Oberlin, he wrote a symphony, a string quartet, and a number of songs for voice and piano, all completed before he was nineteen years old.

In 1942 he joined the United States Air Force. When he was discharged, he enrolled as a composition student at the Eastman School of Music, in Rochester, New York,

where he studied with Howard Hanson and Bernard Rogers. He received his Bachelor's and Master's degrees from the Eastman School and his doctorate from the University of Rochester. While at the Eastman School of Music, Mr. Mennin wrote his *Symphony No. 2*, a "Concertino for Flute, Strings and Percussion," a "Concertino for Orchestra," and a number of songs and piano pieces — quite an accomplishment for someone still going to school.

Mr. Mennin is a natural composer and feels that music must reflect a composer's personality. He follows no particular road or line of experimentation, but rather the classical forms of the symphony and concerto. He says, "The problem which confronts young composers is whether they are using a musical vocabulary which is natural to them and if they can understand it completely. A composer can only express that which he understands; whether the soil from which he has grown is cultured or crude does not matter. He can write worthwhile music if he clearly expresses that which is about him, using words he knows."

Mr. Mennin has been a busy and extremely successful composer. He has had a good share of the available fellowships, prizes and commissions. In 1945 the "Allegro" movement from his Second Symphony received the Gershwin Memorial Prize as well as the Bearns Prize of Columbia University. The next year he was awarded a grant by the American Academy of Arts and Letters and the National Institute of Arts and Letters for his "Folk Overture."

From 1947 to 1958 he taught at the Juilliard School of Music. Although teaching took much of his time, he managed to produce a number of fine works there.

Mr. Mennin has written six symphonies (the fourth, *The Cycle*, for chorus and orchestra, with text by the composer) plus a number of other works for orchestra. He has also written music for band, chamber music, choral works, piano music, a concerto for cello and orchestra, a concerto for piano and orchestra, and a *Sonata Concertante for Violin and Piano*. His works have been presented by many major symphony orchestras in the United States, as well as in South America and Europe. Many of his major works are available on records. The Elizabeth Sprague Coolidge Foundation, the League of Composers, the Robert Shaw Chorale, and the Cleveland Orchestra all have commissioned his work.

Of his own music, Peter Mennin, one of America's most gifted and widely known composers, says, "When someone tells me, 'You must keep your audience in mind,' I answer, 'I write music. If the audience does not understand me immediately, they will later, maybe never, but first I must satisfy myself.' "

Mr. Mennin is tall, dark-haired and dresses impeccably. When asked how it is possible for him to accomplish so much, he smiles and replies, "I word hard, very hard!" And certainly he speaks the truth. His long, busy day allows time for composing, but it must come early in the morning.

When the composer's Fifth Symphony was performed by the Boston Symphony Orchestra in 1951, the music critic of the *Christian Science Monitor* described it well when he said that the piece "comes . . . like a clean, cold and invigorating north wind . . . filled with snap . . . He brings the vigor of his youth, a large measure of originality and the strength that comes from knowing where he is going."

Mr. Mennin has recently been appointed by President Kennedy to serve on the Advisory Committee on the Arts for the National Cultural Center now being planned for the nation's capital.

Gian-Carlo Menotti

born July 7, 1911

Gɪᴀɴ-Cᴀʀʟᴏ Mᴇɴᴏᴛᴛɪ, hailed as the most successful opera composer of our day, was born in Cadegliano, Italy, the ninth child of a family of eleven children. His grandfather was the mayor of a nearby village and his father was in the South American import-export business. He lived with his many sisters and brothers in a large pink villa overlooking Lake Lugano in northern Italy.

Music in the Menotti home was accepted as a natural and normal activity. All of the Menotti children played the piano or some other instrument and from the time Gian-Carlo was in the cradle he was surrounded by music. At the age of four he had already written his first song, and at six he announced that he was going to be a composer. His mother was a fine musician, herself, and she encouraged his musical interests and development. With her he attended many concerts and opera performances.

When the family moved to Milan, Menotti attended the Verdi Conservatory where he studied piano, theory, and composition. In 1927, at the age of sixteen, he came to America and enrolled as a student at the Curtis Institute of Music in Philadelphia. His studies included piano and voice. Rosario Scalero, who became his close friend and

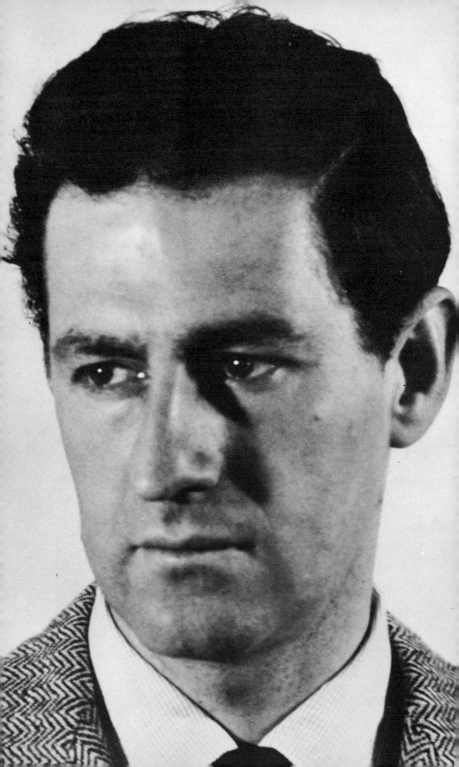

who exerted a great influence on his young pupil, taught him composition.

At the Curtis Institute he also came in contact with many gifted musicians. One of his classmates was Samuel Barber, who became his very close friend, and at whose home Menotti spent many holidays and weekends when school was not in session. During his first year in Philadelphia Mr. Menotti says that he went to the movies three or four times a week, and learned much of his English from the films.

His first opera *Amelia Goes to the Ball* was produced in 1937 at the Academy of Music in Philadelphia and was so successful that the Metropolitan Opera gave performances of it for two seasons in succession. In 1938 Menotti was commissioned by the National Broadcasting Company to write an opera to be produced over the radio. For this occasion he composed *The Old Maid and the Thief,* a comic opera which became an immediate favorite.

Perhaps the composer's first taste of international fame came in 1947 when his serious one-act opera *The Medium* and the delightfully funny opera *The Telephone* were both produced on Broadway. Soon afterward they were performed all over the world.

Another opera *The Consul,* an emotionally gripping story, also made its first appearance on Broadway. It now has been performed in twenty-five different countries all over the world and has been translated into fourteen different languages.

Amahl and the Night Visitors, an opera in one act, was commissioned by NBC Television for performance during the Christmas season of 1951. It has since become a traditional favorite. As operas go, it is unusual because the leading role of Amahl is sung by a boy soprano.

Another of Mr. Menotti's works, *The Saint of Bleecker Street* is one of his more serious works. Altogether, he has written almost a dozen operas and it is interesting to note that in each case he has written the libretto or text as well as the music.

Mr. Menotti is a handsome Americanized Italian who speaks English with a slight accent, but who writes his librettos in perfect English, thinks the English language is ideal for opera, and feels that people should be able to understand what they hear when they attend performances.

Mr. Menotti always takes a very active part in the productions of his own operas. He personally auditions singers to make sure that just the right person is chosen to portray his characters, and often directs the production himself. He is invariably very nervous at performances and fills his notebook with suggestions for singers, orchestra players, stage crew, or for anyone else connected with the production.

Menotti's operatic style is highly original and his music is always used to intensify an emotional or dramatic idea. He is often accused of being sentimental in his melodic line, but it is perhaps his intelligent use of sentimentality which makes each of his operas so very successful. Because of his great flow of melody, Menotti is often spoken of as the successor to the great Italian operatic composer Puccini.

Mr. Menotti is a dedicated artist and an individual. He feels that "artists must be very stubborn and what defeats the artist in America today, is his willingness to compromise in order to achieve success." He is often concerned that a certain melody from one of his works might become too popular. And his greatest fear is that it might be played on a jukebox, his pet hate.

Mr. Menotti is intensely interested in people, which may be the reason his characters are so well defined, so clear and easy to understand. In spite of his love of people, though, this exuberant, hard-working composer sometimes works seven days a week, without a stop. He also is absent-minded, especially when he is not interested in what is going on at the moment. Once, coming back from Italy, he had to fill out some papers for the United States Immigration. In reply to a question about his height, he put down "eleven feet five inches," instead of "five feet eleven inches."

An avid reader, Mr. Menotti is especially fond of horror stories. He is interested in modern art (which he collects), magic and magicians, Italian folk sculpture, and tennis — though he says he doesn't play a good game.

Many of Menotti's important compositions were written in his ultra-modern home, Capricorn, which he shares with composer Samuel Barber in Mount Kisco, New York. His studio is crowded and is just large enough for him and his grand piano. The walls are covered with many modern paintings.

One of his great joys at Capricorn is the bird feeding station where Mr. Menotti feeds and watches many different varieties of birds. He loves animals, especially dogs, and his blond cocker spaniel, Luce, will accompany him on long hikes, or sit outside his door while the composer is working.

Other major works by Menotti include a Concerto for Violin and Orchestra, a Concerto for Piano and Orchestra, and a symphonic poem, *Apocalypse*. He has also written the libretti for the operas *Vanessa* and *A Hand of Bridge* by Samuel Barber.

Douglas Stuart Moore

---

born in Cutchogue, New York, August 10, 1893

DOUGLAS MOORE, one of our very gifted composers, is the son of the publisher of one of America's earliest women's magazines, the *Ladies' World*, of which his mother was editor. As a child he gave little indication that he had any particular interest in music. He attended public school in Brooklyn, New York, and at the age of six started to study the piano.

He went to Hotchkiss, a school for boys in Lakeville, Connecticut, where he showed great interest in academic studies, but it was not until he came as a student to Yale University that he began to study music more seriously. His first songs were written during the time he was studying composition there with Horatio Parker. They were typical college songs popular with students and faculty, but not too serious or important. In 1917, after receiving his Bachelor of Music degree, he enlisted in the United States Navy and, as a Lieutenant, he again wrote songs and musical skits for the entertainment of the Navy men. It was not until his naval discharge that he decided to devote his time to music.

Moore realized that he needed more concentrated study and went to Paris to become a pupil of the well-known

composer, Vincent d'Indy. He also studied organ and composition with Nadia Boulanger.

In 1921 he returned from Europe and was appointed Director of Music at the Cleveland Museum of Art. There he gave organ recitals, lectured on music, and sponsored many musical events at the museum. There were two things that were of special interest and importance to him in Cleveland. One was the fact that the composer Ernest Bloch was director of the Cleveland Institute of Music, where Mr. Moore immediately enrolled in his composition class. The other was the Cleveland Playhouse where he was able to fulfill a desire since childhood to act in plays.

In 1925 a Pulitzer Fellowship made it possible for him to go to Europe and devote all his time to composition. This proved to be a wise decision, because he returned to the United States with a number of fine completed works. He became a faculty member in the music department of Columbia University, and in 1940 he succeeded Daniel Gregory Mason as head of the department. There he remained for thirty-six years, until his retirement in June 1962.

As a composer, Douglas Moore is hailed as one of America's most individualistic and creative artists. He has written orchestral and chamber music, choral works, songs, piano and organ works, and music for films. He has great originality, a fine sense of the dramatic, and a lyrical quality that is hard to match. His early orchestral works, *The Pageant of P. T. Barnum*, the tone poem "Moby Dick," *Symphony of Autumn*, and "Four Museum Pieces," were all written before 1930. The latter work, written in 1922, won him the Pulitzer Prize.

One of his later compositions for orchestra, "In Memoriam," was inspired by World War II and speaks of the waste and uselessness of war. Mr. Moore has also written a string quartet, a "Quintet for Woodwinds and Horn," a "Quintet for Clarinet and Strings," and music for violin and piano.

However, it is as a composer of American operas that Douglas Moore has achieved his greatest success and in this field he will probably be remembered longest. Mr. Moore has said, "I would rather write operas than anything else. To me it is the most spontaneous form of expression. The music writes itself if the book is good."

His first opera, *White Wings*, was written in 1935. He also wrote a delightful operetta for high-school performances, *The Headless Horseman*. His second opera, *The Devil and Daniel Webster*, is a forceful one-act opera written to the poem by Stephen Vincent Benét. When it was performed by the American Lyric Theatre in 1939, it was acclaimed as the finest work in the repertoire of American opera. Next came *The Ballad of Baby Doe*, an American tale based on an actual episode in early Colorado history. It seemed only fitting to have this work performed first by the Central City Opera Company in the tiny rebuilt Opera House of the former "ghost town," Central City, Colorado. It was such a great success that two years later, after having been performed by the City Center Opera Company in New York and on tour, it was again performed at Central City. The composer and his wife were present and lived in a small cabin several miles out of town, tucked in the deep woods, with white-peaked mountains in the distance. He attended rehearsals and performances, watching modestly, and constantly appreciating the work of the singers, orchestra players, and stage and scenery crews.

Now almost seventy, Mr. Moore is a tall, energetic person. He is a scholar who finds literature and art a great source of joy. He has a close association with some of our best-loved American poets and has often used their poems as texts for his compositions. Few children or tourists who stopped to talk to him in front of the Opera House, or while he sat on a worn bench in front of Central City's Teller House Hotel, had any idea that they were speaking to a great man and to a great artist.

The latest of his operas, *The Wings of the Dove*, produced in October of 1961 by the New York City Opera, is unlike his earlier works in that it has no regional setting. Its scope is international, and is based on the novel by the author Henry James. Of this opera, the critic Winthrop Sargeant says, "I am tempted to call it the most artistically successful American opera ever written, and it is certainly one of the very few operas written anywhere in the past half century that seems to deserve a permanent place in the history of art."

Walter Piston

born in Rockland, Maine, January 20, 1894

WALTER PISTON, one of America's most distinguished composers, was born in Rockland, Maine, where he lived until the age of ten. Then his family moved to Boston. Though he studied violin and piano, his real interest was art rather than music, and, on finishing high school, he decided on a career in art. In 1916 he was graduated from the Massachusetts Normal Art School, where he had shown unusual talent in drawing and painting.

During World War I he enlisted in the Navy, and had to learn to play an instrument in order to play in the band. He selected the saxophone, which he learned almost overnight. When the war was over, Mr. Piston earned his living playing the piano and saxophone in restaurants and with dance bands. By this time it was music rather than art that had the greatest attraction for him, and, when he was twenty-six years old, he returned to school to continue his studies. He entered Harvard University, majoring in music, and was graduated with high honors in 1924. A John Knowles Paine Fellowship made it possible for him to study in Europe with Nadia Boulanger.

When he returned from France two years later, he became a member of the faculty of the music department of Harvard University, and there he remained for thirty-

four years, teaching composition to numerous young composers. In 1928 his music was introduced to American audiences. The Boston Symphony Orchestra performed his "Symphonic Piece," the Philadelphia Orchestra played his *Orchestral Suite,* and a well-known quartet played his "First String Quartet."

Walter Piston ranks high among eminent American composers with an impressive list of compositions to his credit. He has written seven symphonies — as well as many other works for orchestra — string quartets, quintets and sonatas, but only two choral works, and no operas or songs. He believes that the fundamental values in music are melody and form. His words are, "The essence of what the composer has to say is found in the melodic thread, which should never falter." Mr. Piston has a thorough knowledge of orchestral instruments and he blends instrumental sounds as an artist mixes colors. He feels that a composer ought to keep in mind the performer or ensemble that is to play his music. He must know the limitations of musicians and their instruments, and must not write music that is almost impossible to play. In his opinion, performance difficulty does not necessarily make a work good.

Basically, Mr. Piston is a "classicist." He has not "kept up" with the times, and he is something of a conservative; but his compositions are very popular and his works probably are played more often than those of any other American composer. Mr. Piston, speaking of his music, says, "It is not one of my aims to write music that will be called modern, nor do I set out to compose according to any particular style or system. I believe my music is music of today in both manner and expression."

This composer has had many of his works commissioned. In 1943 his Second Symphony was commissioned by the Alice M. Ditson Fund, and it was awarded the Music Critics' Circle Award of 1944–1945. Mr. Piston has the distinct honor of being awarded the Pulitzer Prize in music not once, but twice. The first time, the prize was awarded the composer for his *Symphony No. 3*, commissioned by the Koussevitzky Music Foundation. The prize was awarded again for his *Symphony No. 7*.

One of Mr. Piston's most popular works and one which is most often played is his orchestral suite from the ballet *The Incredible Flutist*, which he wrote for dancer Jan Veen. *The Viola Concerto*, written in 1958, received the Music Critics' Circle Award.

As a composer Mr. Piston is a most skillful artist. He knows exactly what he wants to say in his music and says it beautifully. A large portion of his music is instrumental and in large forms, such as symphonies, concertos, sonatas, and orchestral suites. Players enjoy his music as much as audiences do. They always find it interesting and within the range of their instruments and their capabilities as musicians. If they ever have to play his music from manuscript they find it easy to read, for Mr. Piston has had training as a draftsman and artist, and every note on the manuscript is neat and beautifully clear. It is not hard to follow or understand his style or the central theme in his works.

One of his most recent compositions, "Symphonic Prelude," commissioned by the Association of Women's Committees for Symphony Orchestras in 1960, is one of his shorter works. It will be very useful in filling the growing need of the repertoire for short orchestral works. This composition received its first performance by the Cleveland Orchestra on April 20, 1961. As he walked up to the stage to receive the applause of the packed house, Mr. Piston looked much too young to be retired.

Mr. Piston and his wife live in Belmont, Massachusetts. Mrs. Piston, a very skillful artist, devotes her time to painting, while her husband concentrates his energies on composing. His Second Violin Concerto, which is widely performed, was composed since retirement. The composer has recently completed a *Concerto for Two Pianos and Orchestra*.

Mr. Piston is energetic, and there is a real sparkle in his eyes when he smiles. His manner of speech is slow, and his handshake is strong and friendly. Like most people of eminence, Mr. Piston is a humble person. He also has a wonderful sense of humor. A good example of it was his reply to someone who asked why the finale of his Third Symphony was so loud. He answered, "You see, they were drilling an artesian well outside my window, and I had to write music loud enough to drown it out."

Quincy Porter

born in New Haven, Connecticut, February 7, 1897

ALTHOUGH HE WAS THE son of a minister and a professor at Yale Divinity School, Quincy Porter gave no indication that he too might one day become a minister. It was always music that captivated his interests and energy. After having studied the piano for several years, he began at age ten to study the violin, and he showed great proficiency and facility with it. He entered Yale University to major in composition and became a student of Horatio Parker and David Stanley Smith. At Yale, Mr. Porter gave a number of violin recitals, played chamber music, and conducted the university orchestra. When he was graduated in 1921, he was awarded the Steinert and the Osborne prizes in composition.

The following year Mr. Porter continued his musical studies in Paris with the famous composer-teacher Vincent d'Indy and also with Lucien Capet, distinguished violinist and composer.

On his return to the United States, he lived in New York City and played in the orchestra of the Capitol Theater. He continued studying there with composer Ernest Bloch and, when Mr. Bloch was appointed director of the Cleveland Institute of Music in Cleveland, Ohio, Mr. Porter

went to Cleveland with him. He became a member of the Institute faculty, and played viola with the well-known Ribaupierre Quartet. His first two string quartets and his *Sonata for Violin and Piano* were composed in Cleveland.

In 1928 Mr. Porter returned to Paris on a Guggenheim Fellowship, but, surprisingly enough, did not study with Nadia Boulanger, the distinguished teacher of so many American composers. He felt that he did not need a teacher for he knew what he wanted to write and was grateful to be free to do it. Thus, for three years he worked undisturbed and wrote the *Sonata for Violin and Piano No. 2*, which has become a great favorite with violinists and has been recorded several times. He also wrote his "String Quartet No. 3," a *Sonata for Piano*, a most interesting *Suite for Viola Alone*, often performed by the composer, and a "Quintet for Clarinet and Strings." Quincy Porter had emerged as an established composer, one who follows no fads or styles in composing.

On his return from Europe, Mr. Porter became professor of music at Vassar College where he remained from 1932 to 1938. His *Symphony No. 1*, written in 1934, showed a new, fresh vitality found in many of his chamber music works. His very keen ear and his balanced use of strings in orchestral works are often credited to his active participation in chamber music groups. However, judging from the way he uses other instruments, Mr. Porter is equally familiar with all the instruments of an orchestra. His trumpets in an orchestral work are often most unusual and brilliant and his percussion instruments are exotic.

In 1938 Mr. Porter was invited to the New England Conservatory of Music in Boston as the Dean of the Faculty, and three years later he became director of the Conservatory. The years in Boston did not prove very productive, owing to the fact that he was too busy with many administrative duties. When he left the New England Conservatory in 1946, it was to become professor of music at Yale University. His years at Yale have been very creative and have resulted in some of his most important works. His *Viola Concerto*, written in 1948, was followed by "The Desolate City for Baritone and Orchestra" and his *Concerto Concertante for Two Pianos and Orchestra,* which won him the Pulitzer Prize in 1954.

Mr. Porter is considered one of America's foremost composers. He is also recognized as an outstanding violinist and chamber music performer. He has appeared as guest conductor of several major symphony orchestras. His chamber music frequently appears on many programs in Europe and America. In recognition of his contribution to this field, he was awarded the Elizabeth Sprague Coolidge Medal for "eminent service to chamber music."

He has composed more than fifty works for orchestra, chamber music, and compositions for voice and piano. His music is melodic, harmonious, and it does not speak of any particular geographic or national location. Though a New Englander, not one of his works suggests the area. He has, however, written a *Ukrainian Suite* for strings, and a "String Sextet on Slavic Folk Songs." These works were undoubtedly the result of the years he spent at the Institute of Music in Cleveland, a city which boasts a very large Slavic population.

Mr. Porter has recently been appointed Battell Professor in theory of music at Yale University. The Battell professorship, established in 1890, is one of the oldest academic chairs in music in the country. There he is kept very busy promoting and guiding the artistic development of Yale music students who may well be our future composers.

During the summers Mr. Porter and his family go to their home on Squam Lake, New Hampshire, where they live in a comfortable house on the side of a hill. There the composer becomes active in his only hobbies, fishing and making furniture. His workshop is well equipped with wood-working tools, and, when he is not composing or repairing a chair leg, he can be found boating or fishing on the lake. In speaking of his work and his summer home, Mr. Porter says that it is "a sort of MacDowell Colony of my own, but without the colony."

Wallingford Riegger

born April 29, 1885, in Albany, Georgia,
died April 2, 1961, in New York City

ON MARCH 30, 1961, a well-dressed, stately gentleman was walking on a New York street. He was on his way to meet a friend with whom he was to have lunch. He was in no particular hurry and ambling along at a comfortable pace, when suddenly two dogs, leashes in the hands of their owners, lunged at each other directly in his path. It happened too fast for him to step aside, and he tripped on the leashes and fell. An ambulance rushed him to the Columbia Presbyterian Hospital where everything possible was done for his head injuries, but he did not survive the fall, and died on April 2, 1961, at the age of seventy-five. The man was Wallingford Riegger, one of America's leading and most versatile composers.

Wallingford Riegger came from a musical family. His mother was an excellent pianist and his father played the violin and was choirmaster of one of the leading churches in Indianapolis. As a very small boy, his favorite game with grown-ups was to have himself blindfolded and name any note or chord played on the piano. It amazed the musicians who were constant visitors at the Riegger home, but his parents were not at all surprised. Music was a

very normal function of daily living in the Riegger household.

In 1900, when the family left Indianapolis and moved to New York City, they left behind the cellist who played quartets with the Rieggers. Mr. Riegger therefore convinced his son to change from the violin, which he had been studying, to cello, so that the Rieggers would have their own string quartet. Wallingford was most obliging and became a pupil at the Institute of Musical Art, where he studied cello with Alwin Schroeder and composition with Percy Goetschius. Three years later, when he graduated, he decided to continue his studies in Germany.

When he returned to America in 1917, he became head of the theory and cello departments at Drake University in Des Moines, Iowa. During the years that followed, he also taught composition at Ithaca Conservatory, Institute of Musical Art in New York, Teacher's College, Columbia University, the New School for Social Research, and Northwestern University in Chicago. Though he was always busy teaching, Wallingford Riegger was also busy composing. He produced a large number of fine works but unfortunately they were not performed.

To Wallingford Riegger, recognition came very slowly. It was not until he was almost seventy years old that the musical world suddenly realized his magnitude and it was hard even then to place him as a composer belonging to any one special group. His work "La Belle Dame Sans Merci" for solo voices and chamber orchestra was written in the classical tradition, and was the first work by an American to receive the Elizabeth Sprague Coolidge Award for chamber music. The Paderewski Prize was awarded him for his "Piano Trio." These two works led audiences to think of the composer as "sound" — a conservative, rather than a rebel against the traditional or classical form. But then Mr. Riegger surprised everyone with his "Study in Sonority" for ten violins. Here indeed was a change in his style of writing — music of the most extreme dissonance. Wallingford Riegger was writing music using the twelve-tone method!

For some years Mr. Riegger's compositions shocked audiences but now they have become great favorites on concert programs.

He has written a large number of works for the symphony orchestra. His Third Symphony was commissioned by the Alice M. Ditson Fund and had its first performance by the CBS Symphony Orchestra in 1948. It is full of rhythmic vitality, color, and imagination, and the orchestral instruments are used to their very best advantage. It was selected by the New York Music Critic's Circle for its annual award as the most important new orchestral work by an American composer. Mr. Riegger's Fourth Symphony was commissioned by the Fromm Foundation in 1957. "This is a symphony which has both head and heart appeal," is what the critics said about it.

His list of chamber music compositions is long and varied. His *Concerto for Piano and Woodwinds* is a very popular work with chamber music audiences. Mr. Riegger has also written music for band, brass ensemble, piano works, and choral and vocal works. Through the years, the composer also has worked on arrangements of various works for choruses. When his publisher told him that "it was an awful lot of choral music to be arranged by one composer," Mr. Riegger immediately said, "Well, shall I sign another, rather than my own name to these arrangements?" Thus, first as Gerald Wilfring Gore, and later using eight other pseudonyms, Wallingford Riegger made about 400 arrangements of different works, but all of his music has his very own stamp of fine craftsmanship and keen musical intelligence. He was indeed a unique force in the musical life and development of this country.

Riegger's chance meeting with the well-known dancer Martha Graham, resulted in his writing about ten musical scores for leading dancers. Mr. Riegger, a great admirer of modern dance as an art form, found the use of the twelve-tone scale very satisfactory for dance compositions. Themes from his "New Dance," which he composed for the dancer Doris Humphrey, and later arranged for orchestra, is the best known of his dance compositions. Because of his contribution to music for modern dance, he was at times referred to as "America's dance composer."

Wallingford Riegger was a quiet man, modest, rather shy, with an unusual sense of humor. He was vigorous in his appearance and in his music. His energy seemed endless, and the years between his seventieth and seventy-fifth birthdays were the most important of his whole creative career. During this brief period, composer Riegger completed his Fourth Symphony and began work on his Fifth. He also completed a number of small works for various combinations of instruments, and "A Festival Overture," "Quintuple Jazz," and "Sinfonietta," all for orchestra.

In celebration of the composer's 75th birthday, a telegram from Leonard Bernstein, conductor of the New York Philharmonic stated: "It will be my great pleasure to recognize the occasion of Mr. Riegger's 75th birthday by playing a major work of his . . . I regard Mr. Riegger as one of the true 'originals' of our musical culture, and one of the most significant composers." The well-known music critic Alfred Frankenstein said: "Wallingford Riegger must stand high on anybody's list of the major musical figures in the United States . . . His work has been of unique significance from a purely artistic point of view, and his example has been an inspiration to all of us in its lifelong devotion to the twin principals of freedom and creativity."

Although Mr. Riegger was much too busy working to have many hobbies, he did enjoy his garden and was very proud of the landscaping job he did on the grounds of the home in which he lived with his wife in Holland, Massachusetts. He loved to play bridge and was an excellent player. He was also an avid reader, detective stories being his favorite tales.

Wallingford Riegger was buried on the 4th of April, 1961, in Ferncliff Cemetery, Harrsdale, New York. As was fitting, music he had composed was played during the services, the funeral march from his *Sinfonietta*.

William Schuman

born in New York City, August 4, 1910

AT AGE ELEVEN, William Schuman surprised his parents by asking them to buy him a violin. When his father asked him why he suddenly wanted a violin, he explained that he had heard the school orchestra play Beethoven's "Minuet in G" and liked it. He too wanted a chance to play in the school orchestra and perhaps play the piece. His father bought him the violin, never expecting that his son's interest would last, and that he would one day become one of America's foremost composers.

As a boy, William Schuman was an outstanding athlete. He went to the George Washington High School in New York, and was a member of both the boxing and baseball teams. It pleased him immensely to have people predict a great future for him in baseball. Secretly, he had hopes of one day playing ball with the New York Yankees, the Boston Red Sox, or the Cleveland Indians.

He also played in the school orchestra, organized his own jazz band and composed a number of popular songs, but the idea of becoming a professional musician never entered his mind. It was not until he was almost nineteen years old, when his sister, a pianist, took him to his first symphony concert, that he decided to study music.

He enrolled at the Malkin Conservatory of music and

studied harmony with Max Persin, counterpoint with Charles Haubiel, and composition with Roy Harris. At the same time, he was also a student at Teachers College of Columbia University. To support himself during his years of study, he played in a jazz band, worked as a salesman for a lithographer, and wrote the words and music to a large number of popular songs.

The year 1935 proved an eventful one for Mr. Schuman. He was appointed to the faculty to teach music at Sarah Lawrence College, and received a scholarship in conducting at the Mozarteum in Salzburg. In Salzburg he started work on his First Symphony. The next year, it was performed at the WPA Composer's Forum, and though it was well received, Mr. Schuman was not satisfied with it, discarded it, and wrote another one in its place.

He had the same reaction to his First String Quartet, which he also rewrote completely after hearing the first performance. It was not until he wrote his Third Symphony that he began to feel satisfied with the results. This symphony, dedicated to Koussevitzky, was performed by the Boston Symphony Orchestra on October 17, 1941. It was selected by the Music Critic's Circle as the most important work of the year by an American composer.

At Sarah Lawrence College Mr. Schuman taught music and conducted the chorus, but devoted his free days, Wednesday, Saturday, and Sunday, to composing. Some of his major works were written during these years.

In 1944 Mr. Schuman became director of publications at G. Schirmer, Inc., music publishers, and the following year, at the youthful age of thirty-five, became president of the Juilliard School of Music. He worked closely with faculty and students there, and made a lasting contribution to the field of music education. He introduced contemporary music into the curriculum, and practically revolutionized the teaching of musical history, theory, and composition. Because he believed that order and discipline are important in any endeavor, he could successfully combine the job of being a creative artist and administrator of a large school.

As a composer, Mr. Schuman is one of America's best. His music, written in many and varied forms, appears often on concert programs. His cantata A Free Song won for him the Pulitzer Prize in Music. He also received the First Town Hall League of Composers Award for his Third String Quartet. He has written eight symphonies, a number of concertos, several ballets, an opera called Casey at the Bat, much chamber and choral music, as well as other works for orchestra and band. His music shows clear craftsmanship and technique. It is young, vigorous, full of sensitivity and joy. It is well put together and audiences have been very responsive to it.

One of Mr. Schuman's recent works, "New England Triptych," was much influenced by the works of one of our very first American composers, William Billings. It is of interest to note that Mr. Billings, 1746–1800, who was a tanner by trade, wrote mostly choral music. It is seldom heard, yet Mr. Schuman finds in it a deep religious and patriotic fervor, a forcefulness and vigor that is hard to match.

The word "triptych" means a three-paneled picture. Written in 1956, Schuman's work was commissioned by the well-known conductor Andre Kostelanetz who presented the first performance of it. The first movement, called "Be Glad America," is based on an anthem by Billings. The second movement, "When Jesus Wept," is in the form of a round, and Mr. Schuman uses the original music as written by Billings. The third movement is titled "Chester," after a church hymn which was used as a marching song by the Continental Army.

On the first of January, 1962, William Schuman assumed his new duties as president of Lincoln Center for the Performing Arts. The position was both a great honor, especially for anyone as young as Mr. Schuman, and a great responsibility. To the question of whether he still planned to continue composing, Mr. Schuman replied very definitely, "Yes!"

Despite his many accomplishments, Mr. Schuman at fifty-two is extremely youthful. Tall, lean, energetic, looking very much like the successful businessman, Mr. Schuman has learned to use every minute of the day for some useful purpose.

New Rochelle, New York, is home for Mr. Schuman, his wife, and son and daughter. In a small room of the house, he works in the early mornings and during summer vacations. He has set a goal for himself to spend 400–600 hours a year at composing, and keeps a record of the time spent. While working, he is never without his pipe. He works at his desk, rather than at the piano, because he is not happy with his piano playing. "I sing while I write, loudly and badly," he says.

Reading, walking, and swimming are the composer's favorite pastimes, and he finds a brisk swim, or a walk shared with a member of his family, a great help in settling down to compose.

Roger Sessions

born in Brooklyn, New York, December 19, 1896

ALTHOUGH ROGER HUNTINGTON SESSIONS was born in Brooklyn, New York, he is considered a New Englander because he was reared in Massachusetts, and because his family had been New Englanders for many generations. His mother, a fine musician trained in the Leipzig Conservatory in Germany, became his first piano teacher when he was five years old. She soon recognized his remarkable ability as a pianist, but had no idea that his interest would turn to composition.

When he was fourteen years old, the age when most youngsters are ready for high school, Roger Sessions was admitted as a student to Harvard University. It was during his first year at college that he made up his mind to become a composer.

After graduation from Harvard, he continued his studies in composition with Horatio Parker at Yale University. Then during the composer's twentieth year, there were two important events. He won the Steinert Prize for composition with his "Symphonic Prelude," and he was engaged as "assistant" in the Music Department of Smith College, where he stayed for two years. His first major composition, *The Black Maskers*, was written for a Smith College production of a play by Andreyev.

In 1921 Mr. Sessions came to the Cleveland Institute of Music in Cleveland, Ohio, in order to continue his studies in composition with the well-known composer Ernest Bloch, who had become the director of the school. Within a short period of time, his status changed from that of student to that of teacher, or assistant to Mr. Bloch. For four years he worked and taught at the Institute of Music, but, when Mr. Bloch left the city, Mr. Sessions also resigned his position.

A Guggenheim Fellowship and a fellowship at the American Academy in Rome made it possible for Roger Sessions to spend the next eight years in Europe, where he was able to devote all his time to composing. Some of his major works, including his *Symphony in E Minor*, were written during this period. On the composer's return to the United States in 1933, he taught composition at the College of Music of Boston University, the University of California, and Columbia University. Since 1953 he has been professor of music at Princeton University.

Composing and teaching have occupied Mr. Sessions from the time that he was a young man. He is one of the most revered teachers, who feels a deep concern for young composers and spares no time or effort to get their works performed or published.

Mr. Sessions is recognized as one of the major composers of our day. It cannot be said that his music is thoroughly modern or that it follows the Romantic composers. At times, when listening to some of his works, we are reminded of Beethoven's compositions, but, at other times, we find it as modern as the music of the Hungarian composer Béla Bartók or his own teacher, Ernest Bloch. His music is often very serious and intellectual, yet it has great appeal, and expresses depth. He has a thorough knowledge of orchestral instruments, and he creates dramatic effects of "bigness" by their intelligent use. He works carefully and slowly.

His first thirty years as a composer yielded Roger Sessions about ten large compositions. There were two symphonies, two piano sonatas, two quartets, a violin concerto, a duo for violin and piano, his music for *The Black Maskers*, and a one-act opera. It is interesting to note that, as the years progressed, the composer's output grew much greater.

From 1953 to 1958 he wrote a sonata for violin alone, a mass, a forty-minute work titled *Idyll of Theocritus* for soprano and orchestra, a piano concerto, and a third and fourth symphony. Mr. Sessions' influence as a teacher and as a composer is deeply felt in this country and abroad. He was one of six distinguished American composers to visit Soviet Russia as part of a UNESCO project.

Mr. Sessions, his wife, and their daughter Elizabeth live in Princeton, New Jersey. He is a warm, cheerful, and charming person, and at sixty-four he is extremely youthful looking. He demands a lot of his students and tells them that, in order to compose, they must be willing to work hard and have good piano training. "Composing," he says, "is a spiritual thing . . . Technique is not something one learns in school. The composer needs something personal, imagination . . . Musical ideas have infinitely more substance . . . than words can be found to describe them."

In 1961, the music department of Northwestern University had a three-day music festival devoted to the music of Roger Sessions. The composer and his family attended rehearsals and performances. The students who were taking part in the festival were rather nervous to be performing in his presence, but they relaxed after meeting the composer. Then they happily worked harder than ever for the best possible results. "He is so modest and so appreciative of our efforts," was the comment of many of the participants.

Music critic Alfred Frankenstein, in summing up Mr. Sessions, both as composer and man, says, "One of the most fascinating characteristics of Sessions' music is that you expect it at first to be a bit on the academically 'modern' side, and then it comes up and hits you with a terrific amount of juice and steam and a genuine lyric energy."

John Philip Sousa

born in Washington, D.C., November 6, 1854,
died March 6, 1932

JOHN PHILIP SOUSA, known as the "March King," was the oldest of the ten children of a Portuguese father and a Bavarian mother. As is common in many European families, his parents thought that their oldest son should have music lessons and so, at the age of seven, young John Philip started to learn to play the violin. Despite his reputation as being full of mischief, he did very well as a student of the violin. At the end of several years of study, he won five out of the five medals for musical accomplishment in the neighborhood music school. The school authorities felt that they could not give all five medals to one student, and so gave him only three. These Sousa cherished all his life.

One of Sousa's major interests along with his music was baseball. More than once, the young music student got himself into trouble by going off to play a game, thereby being late for a lesson, or skipping it altogether. Once when he was eleven years old, he was scheduled to play a violin solo at school. He also had to play a baseball game on the same day. He played the game, and rushed home to get dressed and ready for his solo. Unfortunately, his mother, who was ill, had not ironed a shirt for him

and he had to wear one of his father's. During the performance, the long sleeves which he had pinned came down and
ruined his solo. His teacher was so cross with him that, at
the reception that followed, he was not allowed to have any
ice cream and cake.

Another time the boy argued with his violin teacher
about his interest in baseball. His teacher would not give
him lessons unless he apologized, and John was not willing
to apologize because he felt that his teacher was in the
wrong. His father told him that unless he studied music
he must find a job, so the boy became a baker's helper.
He lasted at the job exactly three days, and then willingly
apologized to his teacher in order to resume his lessons.

After several years of violin, theory, and harmony,
Sousa's father thought his son should learn to play the
trombone, the instrument he himself played with a band.
John Philip, however, did not make very good progress,
and the neighbors objected so much to his practicing,
that he shortly gave up studying the trombone. Since
his father still felt that his son ought to have some experience playing in a band, he arranged with the bandmaster
to let him play the cymbals and triangle.

By the time he was thirteen, young Sousa, who was
considered a good violinist, organized a small group of
musicians to play at dances and weddings. All the members were grown men, except for John Philip — the only
boy in the group!

It was at about this time that the young violinist was
invited to join a circus band. The idea held great appeal

for him and he had visions of becoming a famous player. He was sure that his father would be very proud of him.

He did not tell his father of the plan, but his father discovered it and, to get the idea out of his mind, immediately enlisted him as a musical apprentice in the Marine Band. While there, Sousa continued studying, began teaching, and at the age of twenty-two became conductor of a small orchestra.

When he was twenty-six, John Philip Sousa was appointed bandmaster of the United States Marine Corps. Under his leadership, the Marine Band became one of the very best and most popular service bands in the country. For twelve years he directed it, until he resigned to organize a band of his own.

Sousa formed his own band in 1892, and he was soon to become very famous. He made many tours of the U.S. and throughout the world. He was well-loved everywhere and the governments of England, France, and Belgium presented him with medals for his contribution to music.

John Philip Sousa composed over one hundred marches. He changed the character of the march from a military gallop or two step to an inspiring and stimulating piece of music. His marches have become the pattern for all marches in America and in many other countries. However, the very first of his marches to be published brought him no money. He gave it to the publisher, who gave him in return one hundred printed copies of it.

Some of his best marches were written while he was Director of the Marine Band. This band is the official band of the President of the United States and plays at all presidential functions. He was not satisfied with the music available and decided to compose other works for these occasions. The results were the "Presidential Polonaise" for indoor White House functions, and the "Semper Fidelis" for functions outside of the White House.

His first march to make a hit with the public was his "Gladiator March," which he sold for thirty-five dollars. After its publication, he did not sell his marches for an outright price, but instead he received royalties or a small percentage of the price of each copy sold. His next march, "Liberty Bell March," earned him royalty payments of thirty-five thousand dollars!

"The Stars and Stripes Forever" completed in Boston, Massachusetts, on April 26, 1897, was originally written for Sousa's band, but has been arranged for symphony orchestra and is just as popular in the concert hall. In 1915, the California Music Teachers Association petitioned Congress to make it — the most popular of all Sousa's marches — the official air of the United States.

Though he is best loved for his marches, Mr. Sousa has also written waltzes, suites, fantasies, and even some comic operas. Few people are aware of the fact that the composer has also written poetry and several books, which never quite equaled the excellence of his music.

John Philip Sousa loved writing music, he loved to conduct it, and, above all, he loved the large audiences who cheered his concerts. He wrote and conducted music for the people, and his marches are real, alive, and stirring.

They are like the composer himself, full of zip and spirit.

His ability to organize and train bands brought a certain excellence to American bands which they might never have had if it had not been for Sousa. He also brought to the foreground certain instruments particularly suited to bands, and made the best possible use of them. One instrument, so very important to the band, was the tuba, but it was almost impossible to carry in a marching band. It was big, clumsy, and heavy.

After much experimentation, Sousa redesigned the tuba in a circular fashion, so that it rests on the player's shoulder with the bell well above his head. The new tuba was much more convenient to carry and is now called the "Sousaphone."

John Philip Sousa was a man of the people. Everyone who knew him loved him. As conductor of large bands, he was never too busy or too tired to talk to children or their parents during the intermission. There was always a twinkle in his eyes, and he loved a good joke.

Sousa's last days were spent on his farm in Reading, Pennsylvania, where he enjoyed his horses and shooting clay pigeons. He died on March 6, 1932, at the age of seventy-eight.

William Grant Still

born in Woodville, Mississippi, on May 11, 1895

WHEN ASKED if there was any one person responsible for his accomplishments as a composer, William Grant Still does not hesitate to speak up quickly, "My mother!" And from what we have learned about his background, he might well have added "and my grandmother." For, from the very day of his birth, he was surrounded by music — sweet soft music sung to him by his mother and grandmother.

His father played the cornet and was the leader of a small neighborhood band in Woodville, Mississippi. When William was less than a year old his father died, however, and he, his mother, and his grandmother moved to Little Rock, Arkansas, where his mother taught in the public schools.

His mother remarried when William was eight years old, and his stepfather delighted the boy with his knowledge, his interest in, and his love for music. His stepfather was not a rich man, but one of the first purchases he made for the family was a record player and a good collection of records. It opened up a new world to William Grant ill. William had no idea there was so much music, and spent every spare minute listening. A short while later,

he was given violin lessons and he was the happiest boy in Little Rock.

Before William had had many lessons, he began making up his own tunes. In order to write them down, he made his own manuscript paper with pencil and ruler. At home or at school, his head was full of music, and he spent every spare moment practicing or composing.

At the age of sixteen, when William had finished high school, he was convinced that he wanted to become a musician. His mother was very sympathetic, but firm at the same time. She was well aware of the problems of earning a living as a musician, especially for a Negro boy, and she insisted that he go to college and study to become a doctor.

He enrolled as a student at Wilberforce College, in Ohio, and, although he was not a music major, he became very active in the musical activities of the college. He composed a number of works for the school orchestra, made arrangements for the band which he conducted, and played violin in the College String Quartet. Instruments of the orchestra fascinated him, and he learned to play the oboe, clarinet, piccolo, saxophone, and cello during his years at college. This knowledge of so many instruments was a tremendous help to him in composing and orchestrating.

Due to a misunderstanding, William Grant Still left Wilberforce College before he graduated, and a period of hardship and discouragement followed. During this time, he played in small orchestras and jazz bands and at times even waited on tables. Finally a small inheritance from his father made it possible for him to study composition at the Oberlin Conservatory of Music in Oberlin, Ohio, and at the New England Conservatory of Music in Boston, Massachusetts. He worked hard but he was not happy with the results of his composition. It was only when he began to study with the noted French modernist Edgar Varèse that he developed a style of his own, and felt satisfied with his musical expression.

Mr. Still is hailed as one of the truly significant composers of our time. His music is a true expression of American life and of the Negro race. He devotes much of his musical energy to the expression and aspirations of his race, for to him Negro spirituals are the most important native American contribution to the world of music. Although he does not draw heavily on spirituals, his music often expresses the feelings, thoughts, joys, and sorrows of the Negro. His *Afro-American Symphony*, and "In Memoriam: the Colored Soldiers who died for Democracy," are a fine example of his devotion to his race.

Mr. Still has written symphonies, five operas, three ballets, and music for orchestra and voices, as well as songs and piano works. He is a highly gifted composer. His melody lines are skillfully drawn, and his orchestrations are colorful and well blended. The composer believes that "one must choose the instrument that best portrays the desired mood . . ."

The composer has had his share of honors, commissions, and fellowships, as well as world-wide recognition. His work "Plain Chant for America, for Baritone Solo and Orchestra" was commissioned for the one-hundredth anniversary of the New York Philharmonic Symphony Orchestra, and was dedicated to late President and Mrs. Franklin D. Roosevelt. In 1945 "Festive Overture" won the composer the Jubilee Season Prize. Most of the composer's works are published and are performed often. In 1936 the composer conducted the Los Angeles Philharmonic Orchestra in two of his own works.

Mr. Still does not feel that he can sit back and "rest on his laurels." He spends at least part of every day of the week composing, and he is unhappy to have to participate in things that mean postponement of his work. He does very little traveling, and finds that social life too often interferes with serious work.

He and his wife, a pianist and the author of librettos for her husband's operas, live in Los Angeles, California, in a small bungalow. His one source of recreation is his well-equipped workshop over his garage, where he makes toys and other small things of wood as presents for grandchildren and little friends.

A deeply religious man, modest, and an independent thinker, William Grant Still belongs to no church, but believes that there is much good in all of them. He believes that his inspiration comes from the Lord, and at the end of every one of his compositions he adds these words:

> With humble thanks to God,
> The source of inspiration.

Picture credits

Aaron Copland	John Ardroin
Henry Dixon Cowell	Sidney Cowell
Paul Creston	Chidnoff
Alan Hovhaness	Louis Ouzer
Ulysses Kay	Hy Reichter
Wallingford Riegger	Henry Verby
William Schuman	Carl Mydans
Roger Sessions	Gerard Studio
Norman Dello Joio	Mia Glazer
Leonard Bernstein	Vandann

NW